Baby Swimming

Lilli Ahrendt

BABY SWIMMING

PARENT-CHILD-SWIMMING DURING THE FIRST YEAR OF LIFE IN THEORY AND IN PRACTICE

With photos by Mathilde Kohl

Meyer & Meyer Sport

Original title: Säuglingsschwimmen
Aachen: Meyer und Meyer Verlag, 2001
Translated by Anne Lammert

British Library Cataloguing in Publication Data
A catalogue for this book is available from the British Library

Ahrendt, Lilli:
Baby Swimming
– Oxford: Meyer und Meyer, (UK) ltd., 2002
ISBN 1-84126-077-0

© 2002 by Meyer & Meyer Sport (UK) Ltd.
Aachen, Adelaide, Auckland, Budapest, Graz, Johannesburg,
Miami, Olten (CH), Oxford, Singapore, Toronto
Member of the World

Sports Publishers' Association
www.w-s-p-a.org

Printed and bound by Druckerei Vimperk, AG
ISBN 1-84126-077-0
E-Mail: verlag@meyer-meyer-sports.com
www.meyer-meyer-sports.com

List of Contents

Baby Swimming

Foreword

Baby Swimming was brought into Germany from the USA by Liselott Diem in the 1960s and was established into the plans for future lectures and research work at the German Sport University.

Since then it has changed its form in many respects. It roused lively interest not only in the newly united Germany but also in European neighour countries, in particular France and the Scandinavian countries, and continued to develop.

Thus the trend towards leisure pools, the building of small pools with warm water, television and radio reports about water births and nimble children in the water, but also scientific reports about baby swimming have triggered off a genuine boom in the range of movement opportunities for babies in their first year: the so-called baby swimming.

The wide variety of different opportunities available faces a great demand for well-informed instructions and expert guidance on the part of parents, clubs, local governments, swimming pool staff, childcare centres. Despite this a universally valid qualification system for institutions offering such courses and for the course instructors themselves still doesn't exist. The German Swimming Federation grasped the initiative last year however with the first instructor-training classes.

This book provides information for both the supply and the demand side on the preconditions necessary, on the behaviour of babies and parents in the water, on secure holding grips and exercises for stimulating movement, the expected effects and the various objectives of early motor stimulation in water. One objective however has proved to be unrealistic, and that is the preparation of young world class swimmers with the help of baby swimming.

Cologne, March 2001
Kurt Wilke

I Introduction

The term baby swimming originates in America, and does not relate to any specific age group other than very young children. It is however possible to differentiate between young children at different stages in their development, and for the purposes of this book the following guidelines are applied:

♦ Baby Swimming: (Up to 12 months)
♦ Young Toddler Swimming: (1 - 2 years of age)
♦ Toddler Swimming: (2 -3 years of age).

The term swimming is used despite the fact that most babies will not be capable of independent motion in the water, but what they are doing relates to the earliest stage in the development of swimming action.

The parents themselves take active part here, by supporting the baby with their hands or by ensuring the baby's head is above the water so as to be able to breathe. The term *Parent-child-gymnastics* in water (cf. GRAUMANN 1996; GERMAN FEDERATION OF SPORTS PHYSICIANS 1994) on the other hand depicts a style of exercise which takes less consideration of a baby's spontaneous movements and the mutual parent-child influence.

Baby swimming represents a parent-child programme of movement under experienced guidance in warm (about 32°) and up to shoulder height water, taught in groups in a playful atmosphere. The lesson which is aimed at early stimulation and the simultaneous pedagogical care characterise the conscious and deliberate actions of the parents with the baby.

Depending, of course, on how well the baby is able to hold up its head, the possible age for joining a course is on average from the 12th week onwards.

Beginning at this time is of advantage as in the first six months – from a neurological point of view – the brain development process is most evident; bonding with a particular person (trust instinct) takes place within this period and the reflex swimming movements are at their strongest. Particularly when baby swimming has been recommended for therapeutic reasons it is then wise to begin with this early stimulation before the baby begins to make strange or throw tantrums; these factors significantly hinder progress.

It is also possible to begin later. One must consider however that in the second six months of a baby's life it starts becoming afraid of strangers and strange places, teething begins, its proneness to illness increases; as the baby is now getting interested in moving forward on the floor and due to its motor skills it is now less dependent on movement stimuli from outside than it was before.

Baby swimming consciously strengthens the parent-child relationship and through early contact with other babies of the same age it furthers the child's development particularly the personality, social and motor skills. As well as this the child's positive attitude to water and the extent of its familiarity with it (cf. JENNER 2000) forms the basis for its enjoyment and overall perception of water (e.g. holidays, shower). This lays the foundation for a child's interest later in learning to swim and complies with the basic principle of teaching swimming – to initiate the learning process by getting used to and coping with the water step by step.

In general a child is not consciously able to learn a proper swimming technique until it's at least three when it has an adequate level of cognitive, physical and motor maturity.

II THE THEORY OF BABY SWIMMING

1 Water

From a chemical aspect water is the bonding of hydrogen and oxygen. It has neither smell nor taste, is transparent and has a faint blue colouring. A human being consists of over 60% water and its life begins in these surroundings in the form of amniotic fluid.

1.1 The Meaning of Water: from a Prime Element to an Element of Movement

Water, a human's *prime element* generally has a phenomenal effect on babies and toddlers. This varied but yet formless element impresses them with its clarity, purity and its pouring and swishing. Because of its thermal and physical chemical qualities this liquid element has always been used not only for cleansing and spiritual refreshment but also specifically for medical and regulatory purposes.

A baby is familiar with water in a special way. In its pre-natal phase it was *lodged safely* in the waters of the womb. Being surrounded by water combined with a great freedom of movement and muscular relief, the skin-intensive stimuli and internal care and devotion from its 'trust person' are some of the possible reasons for a baby's mostly positive reactions when in water.

The medium water offers the baby an entire stimulus-reaction-repertoire; it *answers* the body's movements with changes such as splashing, flowing and frothing. The baby thus perceives itself, its body and its movement to a much more intensive extent than on land.

When it experiences this both delightful as well as self-initiated and causative activity, it is encouraged to repeat the movements, to experiment and to learn. As one can generally see a positive response to water with babies, swimming is classed as being a stimulation for movement development, i.e. as a furthering of movement in water.

Whereas a baby under 'dry' conditions is not able to move itself forward within the first six months and can only raise its head with effort when in prone position leaning on its arms, the three-dimensional freedom of movement in water enables it to move forward with parental support and to test out numerous movement possibilities either repeatedly or in a varied form. Besides, the parent's pulling hand – under the baby's chest at its centre of gravity – allows the baby a more dynamic action with its limbs.

The parental holding under the chest and the resulting pressure effect in the breast zone favours the baby's upright position in the water. Its body assumes a symmetric[1] position, the cervical and dorsal spine are stretched, the shoulder blades[2] and arms are pointing outwards. The legs are out in front kicking alternately. The *reflex locomotion* is particularly stimulated by water splashes and touching the soles of the feet.

Stemming from the VOJTA theory of a *global movement pattern*, *locomotion reflex* as a forming growth stimulant affects the support apparatus and the locomotor system, the central nervous system (CNS) and one's psyche (cf. POTACS 1995). If the *creeping reflex* is stimulated in the prone position, the horizontal muscles are activated and the co-ordination inherent in the CNS is *awakened*.

The elements of these *muscle games* – gravity shift, straightening up, balance shift and the co-ordinated change in the body's actions – are also evident to a certain extent in the deliberate and conscious locomotion patterns which occur later on. So, the co-ordination is activated as well as those muscles for movement patterns (e.g. creeping process), both of which in the normal development process without baby swimming would only occur later. This is due to the necessary confrontation with gravity and the maturity of the CNS.

---

[1]   Even, harmonious.
[2]   Outward movement away from the body axis.

1.2 The Effects of Water on Babies

Physical and sensual impressions change when we are in water. When a baby's body is dipped into water, this triggers off – depending on the development phase-instinctive reflex swimming movements which stimulate the brain activity of the CNS. Being naked intensifies the perception of one's body and its movements and supports the structure of the body scheme.

The extensive touch stimulants through the water resistance stimulate those nerve fibres lying under the skin, creating a relaxing effect regulating muscle tone. This is why babies sleep longer and more deeply after swimming.

A baby experiences its first three-dimensional movement activities in water as opposed to on dry land. It has no problem pulling its legs under its body. These initial *reflex swimming movements (cigarette lighter)* are evident up to its fifth month. They are then replaced by bend and stretch movements a month later and in the eleventh month the movements represent voluntary locomotion – a type of *running movement (cycling)* in the upright position (cf. WIELKI/HOUBEN 1983). The patterns of movement and the upright posture do not differ in principle from motor development under dry conditions. When in water, one's body is open to the influences of physics which have a stimulating effect particularly in those stages of development where a baby is neither able to move around by itself on the ground nor counteract gravity using muscle strength.

The *reflex swimming movements* triggered off by the water enable the baby from to see itself as "independent" from an early age[3]. Prone position offers it a wide visual spectrum of perception. With the help of the parental support in the correct dosage the baby can take on its first targets. The positive cause-effect-relationship of those movements experienced encourage the baby to develop a high level of self-motivation to move. Praise, kind words and protective skin contact all intensify the mother-child or father-child relationship and raise the baby's self-confidence.

Bouyancy force reduces body weight according to the Archimedes principle[4] thus relieving the support apparatus and the locomotor system. Less static muscle strength is needed in water, thus making way for dynamic muscular work.
Another factor here is the light clothing which means that movements are not restricted.

Those parts of the body out of the water need static posture checks. Because the medium water moves by itself the baby's organ of balance is given intensive stimulation to check its own movements and improve them.

A water temperature of 31°-33° [5], perceived as lukewarm, provokes active movement, deepens breathing and activates the cardiovascular system. At the moment of water contact and due to the chest dipping in and out alternately the baby's breathing speeds up; after a good while in the water every breath taken is longer and deeper, the pressure on the chest brings about increased exhalation, the muscles assisting breathing are strengthened which in turn has a positive effect on chest development.

Because of the water temperature and the movement within it, muscle tone is regulated to such an extent that an economisation of movement occurs along with a constant improvement in their co-ordination. A water temperature of more than 33° would relax the muscles and reduce movement impulses.

Friction resistance hinders movement and strengthens muscles. The quicker the movement is and the bigger the surface of offence is, then the higher this resistance becomes which one's body puts up against the water. In the case of inaccurate movement processes e.g. following an accident or due to a handicap, friction resistance can be used for guidance and control.

---

[3] On average in the third month.
[4] Archimedes principle: the body loses an amount of weight which equals that of the fluid which was displaced through its entry into the water.
[5] After 45 minutes in 33° warm water body temperature drops by a maximum of 0.2% (cf. BAUERMEISTER 1984).

1.3 The Quality of Water

"The preventive, medical aspects of swimming are beyond discussion, however the quality of the water in the swimming pool must prove to be 100% hygienic."

(BECK/SCHMIDT 1994, 13p.)

Recommendations for swimming pool water treatment are made by the *Pool Water Treatment Advisory Group* and for indoor swimming pools with water circulation and sterilsation there are specific standards for the quality of water in microbiological, chemical and physical respects.

Bathing and swimming water in public swimming pools for commercial enterprises must not cause damage to human health with pathogens (germs). These requirements similarly apply for hospital therapeutic pools. Similar standards are required for swimming pool water as are required for drinking water and in public and commercially used swimming pools disinfectant (e.g. chlorine, ozone etc) must be used and there should be an adequate system of filtration. The water is disinfected, purified and examined so as to stem the danger of harmful or pathogenic bacteria and inactivate viruses. The staff responsible for the swimming pool technology should therefore test the pool water at least three times a day even when there is automatic dosing of disinfectant and where this does not take place there should be an increased testing of the water. There should also be monthly microbiogical tests of the pool water. The relatively high water temperature (30°C) is recommended and the large number of people in the shallow end, where baby and toddler swimming ideally takes place, means that strict hygenic control is necessary. Hygenic regulations in the form of appropriate examinations also apply to swimming staff themselves in order to be able to guarantee good health for all.

The standards recommended by the *Pool Water Treatment Advisory Group* are as follows:

Microbiological Standards
◆ Colony count – not more than 10cfu per ml
◆ Total coliforms – absent in 100 ml (less than 10 per 100ml is acceptable provided it does not happen in consecutive samples,

there are no Escherichia coli, the colony count is less than 10cfu per ml and the residual disinfectant concentration and pH values are within the recommended ranges).

◆ Escherichia coli – absent in 100ml

◆ Pseudomonas aeruginosa – absent in 100ml.

Chemical Values

◆ Free chlorine – the residual should be at the lowest level that gives satisfactory microbiological quality. This should be possible at less than 1mg/l providing there is an efficient chemical dosing and filtration system. The target where ideal conditions do not exist should be no more than 1.5-2.0mg/l

◆ Combined chlorine – should be less than the free, ideally half or less.

◆ pH – should be maintained between 7.2 and 7.8 with 7.2-7.4 as the target.

Physical Quality

◆ The floor of the pool should be clearly visible and there should be an adequate filtration plant.

Dirt particles such as hair, skin flakes, sebum, body oil, mucus, saliva, sweat, urine, soap rests, cosmetics and micro-organisms (e.g. bacteria, viruses and fungi) or textile fibres which manage to get into the water, stem mainly from our bodies. They are diverted away via the constant flow of water into the processing plant. In order to reduce these sources of water pollution it is essential that all pool users clean their bodies thoroughly. This implies that both parents and babies are obliged to take a shower before entering the water. However as the level of *hygiene awareness* is not always as high as it should be, it is necessary to specifically point this out to course participants in the first lesson, so as to convey and ensure a natural and responsible hygienic attitude on the parents' side from the very beginning and to get the babies familiar with water in a playful and various way (e.g. with the help of watering cans or tubes [6]).

A thorough cleaning of one's body is just as important after being in the water. Showering, rubbing in cream[7] and massaging enhances blood circulation; one's body is warmed up and one's general feeling of wellbeing is enhanced. In order to avoid catching mouth or foot infections, it is advisable to wear flip-flops outside the water; playing materials must be clean.

A person's desire to pass water grows during and in particular after being in the water due to the *Gauer-Henry-Reflex* [8] so that parents are requested to put the baby's nappy on again immediately after showering. For hygienic reasons one should always lay a towel from home on the changing surface.

Although the bins are closed they should be emptied by the course instructor after the lesson so as to avoid unpleasant smells.

---

[6] A tube from a bike or a washing machine which can be pulled and fixed over the showerhead.

[7] Not all creams can be recommended. More information on this in the Öko-test-Sonderheft Kleinkinder (1998) 25 and (1999) 28; this is a German consumer magazine which tests and evaluates goods from an environmental aspect, in this case a special edition on children's products.

[8] Also called Diuresis reflex; The renal passing of water is regulated by stretching receptors in the left auricle. Through the increased amount of blood in the heart the desire to pass water grows while in and shortly after leaving the water, thus resulting in more urination (cf. PSCHYREMBEL 1998, 551; WILKE 1990, 22).

2 The Baby

A human is termed as being a *physiologically premature birth* as the development of brain physiology is not complete when the umbilical cord is cut; the networking of the nerve structure continues up as until the end of the child's second year approximately. The same is true from the aspect of development psychology; being way behind in its movements it is seen as *'hand luggage!'*.

Its sensory organs are not fully matured and its helpless state of being implies a very strong bond – emotionally speaking – to its 'trust person'. Slowly but surely it becomes active and discovers its environment. Its actions and reactions bring delight and amazement thus encouraging its first playful behaviour.

In its first year of life the development of movement involves changing...
◆ from being moved to moving by itself
◆ rom reflex motor activity to one which is voluntary and controlled
◆ from discovering itself to discovering its surroundings
◆ from posture control to movement control
◆ from perception to sensory motor integration[9].

2.1 Physical and Motor Skills Development: from Being Moved to Moving by Oneself

In the pre-natal phase a baby is as closely connected as possible to its mother and is stimulated by movements of the uterus. With the cutting of the cord it speaks for the first time in the form of a loud shout, an expression of its *fear of losing this physical contact*. For this reason, physical or body contact, be it from the mother or the father, is a universal 'soother' for a baby in its first few months. The mother for her part develops a strong sense of perception[10] from the pregnancy, the birth and then throughout the breastfeeding process; she is therefore able to react with the appropriate sensitivity.

---

[9]   The individual perception of the senses are adapted into a superordinate whole and are integrated with each other.
[10] Perceived through senses.

Following the birth the baby shows through its reactions that it is still looking for the kind of protection it had in the womb from new stimuli, and experiences security and instinct trust with physical contact. This protection through body contact is also called the baby's 'earthing' or 'grounding' for all its new forms of experience. Particularly in its first three months, in the so-called 'intentional phase', physical contact is the primary contact experience for the child. In the next three months, the 'oral phase', a visual and acoustic relationship to the mother and father develops.

Physical development

The particular feature of a baby's physical development is a large increase in weight and length, which runs differently depending on a number of things such as hereditary factors, diet and sex. A baby has an average birth weight of 3 000-3 500 g which is doubled by the age of five months and is tripled by the time it's a year. The growth in length runs along a similarly fast scale. A baby is on average 50-52 cm long at birth, at the age of a year it measures 74-80 cm.

In the growing process the physical proportions and appearance change. A newborn baby's head accounts for a quarter of its total body length, an adult's head only an eighth. Arms and legs are short in relation to the body. The growth of the limbs implies a change in the centre of gravity resulting in an improvement in balancing skills. A newborn baby's legs account for a third of the total size compared with a half for an adult. Up until the *first stretch* at the age of five months the knees are constantly slightly bent.

The head proportions are distinctive due to the large cerebral skull and the small facial skull. This formation, together with the chubby cheeks, big eyes and the small body characterises the *child schema* which triggers off affectionate behaviour in adults towards the child.

A healthy newborn child signals that it's breathing on its own through its first shout after the birth. It normally takes 40-50 breaths per minute. For comparison's sake: a toddler breathes 25-35 times in this time, an adult 15-20 times. Its breathing is almost inaudible; it breathes mainly through its nose.

The Theory of Baby Swimming

The development
and functi...
to age...
post...

Baby Swimming

Pulse beat, the pressure wave conveyed ... can best be felt on the inside of the baby ... artery. Within the first six months of life a ... 130 times per minute, from 7-12 months ... and in the second year 90-100 times per ... adult, its pulse rate will have dropped to 60- ...

Blood pressure, i.e. the pressure of the blo... vessels produced by the strength of the card... age. If the systolic (maximal) and diastolic ... rates of a newborn child are still 60/35 mm H ... , will climb to 80/50 mm Hg even within the first year. An adult's blood pressure is about 120/80 mm Hg.

Because of their quick, flat breathing (and lack of concentration), babies and toddlers generally have a weak level of (physical and psychic) endurance. However as their blood circulation can adapt quickly to load, they are able to recover effectively within a very short time.

Development of motor activity

Motor activity includes all processes involved in the steering and control of posture and movement. These processes are a result of varied interaction between sensory, perceptive, cognitive and motivative events[11] (cf. BAUR/BÖS/SINGER 1994, 17). The development of motor activity is based on innate reflex mechanisms, which as a continual consequence of learning opportunities and through interaction with the sensory-motor systems divide up (differ), arrange (structure) and simultaneously bundle up (centralise) to select a partial function. Perceiving and moving are seen as a *biological unit*; perception and movement on their own are inseparably connected according to WEIZSÄCKER'S *Gestaltkreistheorie* (1950).

---

[11] Events which, through the sense organs' functional intake (sensory), through perception and recognition (perceptive), through desire (motivative) and through processing (cognitive) supplement the child's knowledge and guide him to conclusions.

ment of motor activity refers to the processes of control on for posture and movement and how they work according. The function processes are linked systems. However static ure control, through muscles or through balance, is always the prerequirement for more complex dynamic movements. As regards muscle and movement perception – from a kinesthetic point of view – there are three phases: the development of body schema (awareness of one's body, the body's limits, body parts and movement abilities), of balance (feeling for positioning and movement, holding and placing reflexes) and the situational orientation. Movement perception develops slowly; the first real balance reactions can be seen from the sixth month on.

Motor activity development runs in different phases *(neuro-, sensory and psychomotor phase)*. Characteristic here is the appearance and disappearance of various reflexes and movement patterns as well as different levels of awareness. If a reflex in a particular development phase continues longer than it should, or if it doesn't come at all, this often points to a delay in development or a disturbed change in movement behaviour. The sensory motor learning processes in the first year are to be seen as adaptation processes to environmental conditions i.e. the organism adapts and modifies itself to stimuli according to the *principle of homoeostasis* – body functions remain in balance. Adaptation takes the form of an improved tolerance of a stimulant (getting used to it = habituation), an improvement in co-ordination or a higher performance capacity.

During the process of motor activity development a baby attains movement skills which are a result of practising, learning and varying movement patterns and perceptions, the putting together of individual movements with non-motor functions (room orientation, its own picture of the movement, logical combination, decisions) as well as other mental 'digestive' processes through adjustment *(accommodation)* and adaptation *(assimilation)* (cf. PIAGET 1996). Thus movement performance does not evolve from the primary movement skills (e.g. speed, strength) but is learnt as a movement structure; these structures gradually extend to become strong, variable, complex control performances as the intake, processing and output of information becomes increasingly more efficient.

In a baby's first year the motor development is roughly divided into two phases: *the lying phase* for the first six months approximately where it is principally moved passively by being held, carried and transported; this is followed by the *locomotion phase* where a baby is actively interested in getting around on its own. This activeness is clearly noticeable in its second year.

The development runs in two basic directions: *cephalocaudal,* i.e. from the head downwards to the end of the spine, which is easy to identify e.g through a baby's efforts to try and get upright; and *proximo-distal* i.e. from the trunk towards the fingers ranging from movement co-ordination near the body to control ability for things further away, e.g. how a baby touches, grasps and handles certain objects. The initial oversized arm movements out of the shoulder joint in a bid to grasp some object are followed some time later by individual finger movements for picking up crumbs off the floor.

All motor actions that a baby makes under dry conditions are aimed at balancing posture and movement against gravity and controlling them. A baby continues developing these skills. In the first months of its life one can notice in the carrying out of its movements a strong accompanying movement by the leg/arm on the opposite side (contralateral movements) as well as a high level of muscle tension (hypertonia), e.g. in the form of waving and window-cleaning movements.

In the lying phase (0-6 months) the body begins the process of setting itself upright by lifting the head when the baby is laid into the prone position. In supine position the baby observes its hand and puts them in its mouth at around 3 months. The legs can change from a bent position to a stretched one. Through increasing kicking and support movements of the legs as well as a sidewards turning of its head, the baby tries to turn onto its stomach (approx. 6 months). The prone position helps it learn to move around on its stomach and with the support of the upper arms and the pelvis it learns the position on all fours (approx. 8 months). If it shifts its weight to the side it can manage sitting sideways to get out of the horizontal position into a vertical one.

It tries out and learns crawling forward by itself. With the help of stable objects it eventually reaches the upright position (approx. 10 months). By carefully holding on e.g. to furniture, the child practises moving around in an upright position balancing and swaying (approx. 11 months) and it tries to stand on its own for a second (approx. 12 months). At about 13 months it carries out its first independent steps.

The development of a child's motor activity runs as follows
(cf. MEINEL/SCHNABEL 1998, 240):

Age	Phase ...	Description of movement
0-3 months	aimless mass movements unconditioned positional and movement reflexes	◆ Lying age (supine position): grasp reflex, labyrinth reflex (attempt to raise head), stride, climb, crawl, swim reflex, up to the second month a strong bending tone, kicking of the legs, window-cleaning arm movements, focus on objects, discovery of the hands
4-12 months	learning of the first co-ordinated movements	◆ Up to 6 months: lying age (supine position): conscious grasping, propping up onto lower arms and hands, knocking of hands, shifts in balance. ◆ From 7 months: baby begins to move forward horizontally (prone position): spinning around, quadruped position, crawling, creeping, getting into sitting position, walking along or pushing of objects, tweezer grip, pincer grip, hitting objects against each other and letting them fall.

The central nervous system (CNS) and muscle tone

The brain stem, the lower cortex and the nucleii inside (stem ganglia) are already structurally differentiated and mature in function when a baby is born full term. The cortex and the cerebellum are only completely mature for function after a multiplication of nerve cells and their dendrites, which develop quickly in the first two years of life. A baby's movements are initially controlled by the stem brain and later by the cortex (cf. LIETZ 1993, 16; MICHAELIS/NIEMANN 1999, 19ff.).

Muscle tone develops in compliance with the maturing process of the nerve structures. A full-term newborn child shows slightly more muscle tension (hypertonic phase), the so-called *infant stiffness*; Bending muscle activity (flexor activity) is stronger than that of the stretching (extensor) activity. Movements alternate rapidly, partly with strong muscle tension, partly long substantial and intensive movements, and then suddenly in reaction to all stimuli. The legs kick in alternation, the arms are busy waving. The innate positional and movement reflexes are controlled by the lower cortex without inhibition emitting from the cerebrum. Towards the end of the second month more and more stretching muscle tension (extensor tone) develops. The peak of this stretching tendency occurs between the fifth and the seventh month of life. The functions of the cerebellum and cerebrum half-sections are becoming more mature all the time, movements are selected and muscle tension returns to normal.

Setting the body upright

The process of lifting its own body against gravity up out of the horizontal position depends on both a baby's muscular strength and body weight as well as on control and motivation. In the womb the baby's spine was under permanent stretched tension, the so-called *total kyphosis*. Even after the birth it is still very rounded. A baby has the urge to become upright in prone position at first and begins to lift its head (erection and lordosis of the cervic spine). In the process it gains strength in its back. The whole procedure continues – still in prone position – with the lifting of the shoulder and pelvic girdles (dorsal erection and kyphosis).

Through the move up into a standing position and with more and more walking the pelvis tilts forward and straightens up (erection and lordosis of the lumbar spine). The stress on the foot from standing (alone) and walking means that the plantar arch is raised. The upright movement enhances the development and practice of balancing skills. They are in turn responsible for controlling and regulating unaided sitting and walking. The balancing organ in the inner ear (vestibular apparatus) analyses the body's position in the room and stimulates it through changing rhythms of movement. These in turn influence the tonic and vegetative reflexes i.e. muscle tension and the CNS.

Intelligence development

The first phase of the development of intelligence up to i.e. 18 months is referred to as the *senorimotor intelligence* phase. This neuro- and *sensorimotor* phase is characterised by incomplete but independent locomotion on two feet [12], a marked oral phase and the acquirement of *practical* intelligence. The acts of intelligence are rooted in a combination of feeling, perception and movement and are carried out without much reflection or visualisation beforehand. Thinking, moving and acting is a learning process of six phases.

The inherent reflex mechanisms are the first to be exercised. Then in the second month simple habits come into being e.g. in the form of sucking fingers *(primary circular reactions)*. Between the third and the seventh month a baby develops its first adapted movements which are actively repeated and which include objects *(secondary circular reactions)*. From the eighth up to the twelfth month a baby's actions are already co-ordinated, conscious and deliberate; the first combinations of aim/means and if/then can be noticed here as well as the discovery of the cause and effect relationship.

---

[12]   Average walking age in Germany is approx. 13 months.

After the child has extended its methods of action in the active experimentative phase *(tertiary circular reaction)* at the age of 18-20 months it no longer needs many practical solution attempts as it is already able to visualise solutions. It is implementing its sensory-motor intelligence (cf. PIAGET 1996).

Reflexes and movement behaviour

Primitive reflexes and the simplest posture and movement patterns which are already inherent in a child are increasingly replaced by more complicated, combined patterns of action and movement processes within the first year of a baby's life. In this period a baby develops its movements in a continuous process of a combination of differentiating, centralising and control. The sensory motor stimuli are combined under the control of several sense organs e.g. through observation and sensitivity for surface and depth. According to individual aptitude a baby's movements become more complex as it experiences more and more about itself and its surroundings. Sensory motor information on feeling of balance, on its ability to react and on its situative ability to adapt are all tuned in with each other at an optimal level so as to achieve stability in its movements. *Motor skills* come about through the senses' experience (visual, acoustic and tactile awareness), body experience (the ability to visualise trunk, head and extremities in structure), experience with dimensions (gross motor skills) and small scale experience (fine motor skills).

In the first three months postural, movement and balance reactions are essentially triggered off locally by balance receptors in the inner ear as well as by organs of sensation in the cervical muscles, in that the head position towards the rest of the body changes or the body as a whole in a room changes. General static reactions are the tonal cervical and labyrinth reflexes and the combined reactions. Local touching triggers off separate static reactions (crossed stretch reflex, grip reflex of the hands and feet, flight reflex, glabellar and gallant reflexes) as well as support reactions of the legs. Righting reactions are achieved through sudden changes of position; they occur for postural orientation reasons. These individual reactions are the labyrinth, cervical and righting reflexes, the clutching (moro-) and lateral position reaction, the willingness to jump and the bend-stretch reaction (Landau reaction). Holding, righting and balance reactions ensure a correct body posture when the body position has changed and bring about compensatory and accompanying movements so as to maintain one's balance. These reactions start developing in prone position and perfect themselves later on through sitting and standing.

A child up to three months possesses an involuntary kicking motor activity which can be seen in the form of an uncoordinated surplus of movement. When lying in prone position in water, a baby up to five months shows strong, rhythmic alternating leg movements. The arms are generally not as active, they are wiping and waving on the side. The more intensive leg movements evident in babies can be explained by the law of *cephalo-kaudal* development, i.e. from the head down to the feet: in the first five months reflex movements are inhibited in their voluntary activity from the head down towards the feet. The trunk tilts sideways towards the flexed leg (amphibian movement).

From the fourth month up to the end of its first year of life the child learns its first *coordinated* movements. Orderly movements occur firstly around the mouth and eyes, then with the entire head, the arms, hands and fingers (*proximo-distal* direction of development). The development continues in the direction of the feet (*cephalo-kaudal* direction of development). The flow in coordination is thus converted through turning the head and the body, propping up, grasping, crawling and cross-coordinated creeping; towards the end of the first year this flow becomes more differentiated and specific. The child's original voluntary movement processes are worked on and picked up by the baby itself and then practised. They are then controlled consciously.

2.2 Sense Organs and Perception: from Stimulus Intake to Sensory Integration

"Perception precedes every movement. Before a person learns how to move, he must be able to feel".

(ZINKE-WOLTER 1994, 50)

The environment offers the child sensual stimuli which are taken in by the nervous system like *food* and are processed into adaptive reactions so as to develop both body and mind. In this way the child in the first few years of its life learns to direct its attention, to carry out its movements accurately and to control its feelings (cf. AYRES 1992, 16ff.).

The development of the senses within the first year can be summarised as follows:

◆ *Seeing:* The eye is the poorest developed organ in a baby. A newborn baby's visual acuity is slight. At the age of a year it amounts to 35% of that of an adult, at the age of two 50% and at the age of four it reaches 75% of an adult's visual acuity. It is fully developed by the age of six. The optimal distance for observing an object is about 20-30 cm. Focussing of an object and hand-eye coordination are required for conscious grasping. While babies are only able to recognise contrasts at the beginning, a three-year-old can clearly identify visual and linguistic differences in colours. A child of four years can see and describe three-dimensionally, and can estimate short distances.

◆ *Hearing:* From the very beginning the reaction to acoustic stimulus is good. A baby finds it particularly pleasant to be lying at the mother's heart and to hear her heartbeat which is so familiar to it from its phase in the womb. In its first year a baby learns to differentiate between emotional states by the sound of a voice. From acoustic learning and rhythmic experiences the language faculty is developed. The child likes to produce sounds.

◆ *Touching:* The skin's tactile reactions to heat, cold, pressure, pain and touch are fully developed and present from the very beginning. The sense of touch is the dominant sense in the first two years of life.

The most important organs of touch here are not just the hands but also the mouth.

◆ *Smelling/Tasting:* A baby's sense of smell is sensitive from the beginning and the sense of taste is also well developed.

◆ *Sense of balance:* Vestibular perception, the feeling for movement, acceleration and change of position is regulated by the semi-circular canals of the inner ear and a baby begins with this already in the womb. After the birth it would still prefer to be moved around and for this reason the best way of calming a baby is when it can feel rocking, swinging and jumping movements. The first balance reactions in the form of head positioning reaction and support movements can be seen from the sixth month on in general.

◆ *Sensation of movement:* Kinesthetic perception, which is closely linked to vestibular perception, takes in sensations of pressure and stretching stimuli through 'feelers' in the muscles, tendons and capsules. The baby answers with reactive movements, which only begin to differ from each other over the first year and change from being reflex-controlled to voluntary answers in movement.

From the sixth week up to the sixth month, the *critical* phase in which a child's perception develops particularly intensively, the mother-child relationship sustains its influence as the baby's awareness is at a practising stage. The baby reacts to particular signals and stimuli of body language (especially those indicating change of position, i.e. stimulating sensitivity for depth in the form of egocentric communication)[13]. The signs and signals that a baby perceives and takes in during the first months of its life refer mainly to balance, muscle tension, posture, temperature, vibration, skin and body contact, rhythm, speed, pitch of voice, tone colour, resonance and sound.

The development *of perception* occurs with the maturity of the sense organs which allocate and process intaken stimuli through intellectual and brain physiology (sensory motor integration). This process of *perceiving and comprehending* already begins in the third month of pregnancy with the first sensations of touch, and continues for about 8 years until the development and integration of perception is completed. It moulds the basis for the child's entire intellectual and social development as well as that of its personality.

In the first two months a baby's attention is short-term, it is not yet able to cope with the abundance of stimuli. From the third month on it begins to combine individual sense regions. It only gradually improves its ability to perceive with its senses. At first it takes in its surroundings through its 'near' senses.

These senses include skin sensitivity, body and movement awareness, balance and taste. Stimulating these senses is of prime importance for sense development in babies, as the brain is of *extodermal*[14] *origin*. Stimuli for the organ of balance are considered to be of particular significance, as they are among the earliest sensations in a person's biological development. This explains the initial priority treatment of the 'near' senses for a baby. Touching the skin is of special importance: tactile perception reports fundamental, qualitative information about muscle tension, room orientation and the upright position to the cognitive brain function. This is why being naked enhances a baby's intake of movement information.

Within the first six years and as the child gets older the *'far'* senses such as seeing, hearing and smelling are preferential for perception and overlap the 'near' senses.

---

[13]   Self-centred view of the world, the baby sees itself as the centre of attention.
[14]   The supply with nerve stimuli which enters the body from outside through the skin.

2.3 Mother and Child, Symbiosis to Independence

Particularly in the breastfeeding phase a strong, emotional link occurs between mother and child, isolating them from third parties to a certain extent. For this reason their relationship is often referred to as 'shared egotism'.

It's during this critical phase that instinct trust, impetus and hope are developed. The baby sees its mother as a 'secure base'. With her visible and audible presence she gives it the essential support in its bid to discover the world.

As the baby's interest in its environment grows and its ability to express itself increases the parents become active; they influence their child's oncoming motor, perceptive and vocal activities and skills by compensating its insufficiently controlled motor activities, by rewarding it for achievements or by either imitating or showing it actions. This support and furthering makes way for further stages of development.

Physical closeness implies food for the baby's wellbeing. If this mother-child-interaction is disturbed, the child's development suffers, particularly in the cognitive and social-emotional fields. The baby looks for emotional security and symbiotic[15] protection and it needs to communicate and perceive with all its senses. In order to fulfil these needs it must rely on them being conveyed through one or several persons. The trust person's communicative skills and perfected abilities influence a baby in its adapting, learning and practising processes without the parents even being aware of it.

The typical forms of parents' adaptation to infant needs include participating, compensating, motivating, rewarding, imitating and setting an example.

---

[15]   Making use of each other in life together.

This regulation of behaviour is also very important in the early interactions between parent and child when trying to find out soothing methods. After being born the initial period of a child's development is low in stimulus. Many of its movements are triggered by reflex. The short times that it is awake and the wearing physical adapting processes tire it out quickly. Therefore being carried and rocked by its 'trust' person is a welcome piece of vestibular and tactile physical encouragement.

Parents recognise many of the inconspicuous key signals in their child's behaviour and they answer these signals practically out of coincidence be it visually, vocally, through facial expression or motor activity, thus encouraging the child's independent, deliberate behaviour as well as its self-perception. In order to regain security in a new, unknown situation it looks for cover from its mother so as to orientate itself to her signals (facial expression, language). She in turn unconsciously conveys her own reactions and attitudes to the surroundings. Her behaviour is of consequence as the baby builds up a picture of the world which she has conveyed to it. Experiments carried out observing children's 'finding out' behaviour towards a neutral, unknown object showed that a mother's positive or negative (facial) expression proved to be *contagious*. A frightened expression had longer-lasting effects than one of pleasure (cf. PAPOUSEK/ PAPOUSEK 1990, 526).

In the second six months of life a child attaches itself to the person mainly responsible for its care (mostly its mother), a so-called *specific attachment*. In order for the mother-child-bonding to remain intact, the decisive factor is how the mother reacts to the baby's needs from the very beginning and to what extent she takes up social contact with it.

Mother and child form a *stimulus-reaction unit* having mutual influence. The mother's moulding influences are directed towards the developing baby who is lively and quick to react, i.e. an exchange takes place. The baby's striving efforts towards its person of trust is obvious. Success-oriented behaviour is repeated (trial and error) and intensified through reward and punishment.

While on the one hand a 'tendency' exists from mother to child, on the other hand the baby attracts its mother so strongly that she is inevitably captured by its spell. The mother's own personal emotional system is moved to such an extent that she is sucked in by the baby's reactions and has to "resist all varieties of temptation which the baby has on offer" (SPITZ 1967, 143). From a psycho-analytic view she is the observer of its *innocent* activities, she experiences and tolerates the childish behaviour and in the process her own childhood memories, fantasies and struggles come back to life. Pleasant activities for her are encouraged, unpleasant however are rejected.

A mother's *unconscious* actions bring her a huge amount of relief – she is set free, encouraged and pushed forward. They are directed towards her 'ideal ego' whereas *conscious* demands are closely related to her 'over ego'. A mother's gift of empathy is orientated to how she perceives her conscious and unconscious desires.

Significant characteristics of the early mother-child interactive phase of body language are the *'tonic'* *dialogue* and *'tonic'* *empathy,* i.e. important signals are exchanged not only through voice and sound, but also through posture, muscle tension, state of balance, temperature, vibration, skin and body contact and rhythm.

In its first year a baby develops out of the passive state of being moved to moving by itself. Being moved by its 'trust' person, as a rule the mother due to the birth, is the child's primary experience of movement. By being moved and without getting active itself, the baby practises orientating itself in the room and differentiating between certain movements. Moving out of the room is associated with this and implies simultaneously moving away from its mother. What seems to be perfectly natural for the child is often hindered by mothers in particular, afraid that the child is turning away from them; they underestimate the child. This important strive to go and discover occurs more frequently at a later age when the baby is already able to move around by itself and try its luck climbing something for example. In baby swimming mothers act in various ways; having been given ideas and hints for movement, many conduct the movements themselves intensively, others hardly at all, and a further group move their babies intensively. Some don't demand any movement whatsoever from their baby but rather seem to just want to be near it and protect it.

In highly civilised countries, women's physical habits can be considered to be a good distance away from their actual body due to their daily dressing habits, the frequent outer influence on 'ideal' appearance as well as cultural requirements. A critical comment here: in old traditional African, Asian and South American tribes, massaging the baby daily and carrying it everywhere, close to its mother, skin on skin no matter what work is to be done, is routine procedure (cf. LIEDLOFF 1999). The baby is constantly moved around and thus physically stimulated.

Studies of African children showed that these babies are further developed than the Europeans. It seems reasonable that this closer relationship between mother and child can be one responsible factor for this quicker development. African mothers carry their child around with them at all times and breastfeed them for example as soon as they start to cry. This close cooperation shows that it may be possible to alter a child's behaviour through learning processes but a child's development primarily depends on the emotional atmosphere between mother and child.

Another brief digression: From observing monkeys one could identify extreme variations in the mothers' nursing behaviour: the mother's temperament had a strong influence on the baby monkey's movements. A nervous, edgy and easily confused mother can often frighten her child with sudden and (for it) unexpected movements.

Experience also plays a decisive role in the way a mother is with her child; these differences have been demonstrated with first-time mothers and those who already have children. The latter are considerably more easy-going and confident with their children. It has been proved that balanced encouragement from the mother has a greater effect on a baby's development than the abundance of physical surroundings and the number of toys.

Mother-child interaction can also be disrupted in progress. The communication between parents and their child can especially be endangered when problems in development occur, e.g. in the case of a *difficult* baby *(bawler!)*, or a baby who is behind in its development or even potentially handicapped. It is often difficult to decipher these babies' behaviour which is characterised by frequent negative expressions of feeling: they avoid social contact, are easily disturbed and often unpredictable, they scream more often and are hard to calm down. As a result the intuitive communication is derailed and a state of parental failure sets in with feelings of powerlessness and guilt. This in turn can bring on a feeling of despondency as the child has not been accepted innerly. Typical symptoms of this are e.g. a reluctance to answer (responsiveness), increased evidence of 'steering' and insisting on sticking to the rules (dirigism), as well the avoidance of playful dialogues. From a common sense side of things what can set in instead in the parents' heads is a steered, performance-oriented form of training of individual skills which in turn only hinder socially open-minded behaviour.

The secure mother-child-bonding with relaxed, unforced child development can also be disrupted by a number of potential burdens which can only be listed in note form here: parents can cause a negative change in their relationship with their child through personal psychic illnesses, unsolved psycho-social conflicts, bad childhood experiences, real and neurotic fears of the child not being able to survive, early separations as a result of a premature birth, premature rejection of the child, severe states of exhaustion, exaggerated *top-heaviness* and performance orientation or insecurity. The parents here can be dominated by their own problems to such an extent that the willingness to behave intuitively is inhibited. This is noticeable when they avoid playful contact with the child, overhear its signals and neglect its needs or when they tend to over-stimulate the baby.

Being together with their child in the water enables an intensive physical communication with the child through the skin. Touching is an expression of affection. The normal interaction between mother and child, which is conveyed by means of the sight-related so-called *proto-communication* through the mother's facial expression and melody of speech (cf. KARCH 1994, 136ff.), is expanded in water through communication of the entire body. This demands a great deal more sensitivity from the parents in the water than in everyday situations, as the child's trust and mood depends on how they hold and support it.

Mothers unconsciously carry out many patterns and forms of interaction, i.e. instinctively, spontaneously and apparently without planning. In contrast to this are the planned, deliberate interactions, e.g. taking part in a swimming course or ritual forms of play or action where the adults deliberately control and guide the baby's movement development. The lesson situation in Baby Swimming is based on a common and communicative togetherness in which all participants should feel comfortable in an unforced atmosphere. Particular attention is paid here to the children's, adults' and interactive *body language*, partly due to being (almost) naked, the parents' support in securing the baby while swimming and the medium of water – near to the body and frequently unfamiliar. Not only certain insecurities in one's body behaviour come into being here but new interesting possibilities of interaction also develop between the parents and the baby.

2.4 Behavioural Change - from Play and Discovery to Learning

If one should happen to pose the general question as to why children play, one could come up quickly with many, different reasons:

Children play in order to...
- have fun
- pursue their interests and preferences
- express their aggression and interests
- to cope with their fears
- to gather material and personal experience as well as to
- develop social contact and communication.

Even in the womb the foetus put its thumb into his mouth. This urge to discover, to find out about the shape, size and surface of objects is still very evident in the first year of life. For psychological development reasons a baby begins to play with its own body. Because of the limited ability to carry out conscious or accurate movements, head, limb and tongue movements are the first actions which are initially repeated.

If the baby's trust person comes along and does something in front of it and/or imitates it, this activity can intensify and become an interactive game. In the first six months a baby discovers its hands, its stomach, its legs and feet and guides them towards its mouth or kicks them against whatever it's lying on. It is interested in faces and wants to touch them. The deliberate gripping and letting go is still hindered by the hand reflex at the beginning. This reflex disappears during the first year. Playing activities with a lot of emphasis on the body are suitable for this age: e.g. rocking and swaying games, massaging and touching games, gymnastic exercises for the arms and the legs, play with music and sound and games using facial expression.

By touching its body, particularly its feet, the baby develops more hand grasping skills, as a prerequisite for coping with certain objects in its hands. At the age of about six months it is increasingly interested in manually examining objects, such as grasping, hitting and throwing them. This infant form of play is referred to as *functional play*. It begins from the sixth month onward and dwindles by the age of 2-2.5 years of age. Characteristic for this first playing phase is random playing with both uncontrolled as well as impulsive and even orderly movements. The child loves repetition and it uses up its high functional desire and delight at its own activity. From the seventh month on the baby begins to look at objects more closely and examine them. Now babies are enthusiastic about tickling, drumming, rattling, clapping, flying and falling games as well as for watering can activities.

Basically one can say that a child in the process of the first two years of its life discovers objects orally, manually and visually. In this way it develops its ability to picture things three-dimensionally.

The playing situation at baby age consists of 'free' or spontaneous play. It is characterised by joy, unproductiveness, the willingness and involvement of those playing as well as the relationship to 'non-play'. This does not mean that playing is just a casual activity, but rather refers to the work-intensive stage of 'concentrating and mentally coming to grips with something' i.e. learning.

One should offer the baby things to play with so that it can examine them in peace. If a game is interrupted by its parents although it was still contented playing it demonstrates this with expressions of displeasure and demands an alternative. Playing requires inventive problem-solving and, at a later age, communicative or common action. In this respect playful approaches with children go hand in hand with life in society and mental development. Free play with open tasks and with selected playing material promotes creative thinking.

Well planned forms of play also support creativity by giving playing and learning ideas depending on the stage of development. Within a group it is possible to arrange games in which the babies are required to fulfil some demands. Lesson and group ritual games, noted for being carried out playfully and together, develop into a fixed form of play.

Playing within a group is of special importance for the child to the extent that the intensive physical activity, the observing of the other players and the *contagious* happiness through the others all go to enhance the baby's involvement, its eagerness to participate and the final results.

As regards the situation in water, playing is an intensive form of parent-child interaction. At the beginning the baby's intake of the adults' play-oriented attention is passive (eye contact) to a large extent, although most of the time it already answers with a facial expression such as a smile. By repeating activities such as sounds, facial expressions and movements a play situation develops between the parents and the child where the child's reactions are more and more active.

From a social point of view, the baby still plays preferably by itself, but from time to time already demands its parents' attention. When together with other babies it plays contentedly as long as it doesn't feel disturbed. It only lets go of interesting objects when another object is visually more stimulating. In the process of the first year a baby adapts to objects through its eagerness to discover and its improving manual skills; a process which is based on experience and depends on maturity.

Playing with things

To play with objects a baby requires visually guided grasping and appropriate interaction between eye and hand as well as the mental recognition of an object, i.e. the certainty that it exists even if it suddenly disappears for a while *(permanency of objects)*. The child *learns* that through its fine motor skills it can change the movement patterns necessary by repeating 'research' processes with objects in numerous ways.

Depending on age and level of development various objects are suitable as toys. In the first year these would be 'biteable' items that produce noise. Towards the end of this year the baby can already co-ordinate several objects: small ones are emptied into bigger ones and out again, building block towers are built and then knocked over, a rolling ball is a real challenge for a baby. Interactive forms of playing develop between parents and their child (e.g. hiding games and finger activities, catching games). Horse-riding games, singing and movement activities all encourage the child to react, which it does, sometimes intensely (letting off steam).

Baby Swimming

3 Parents and Course Instructors

3.1 Parents as Learners and Go-Between for Their Child

The growing demand for courses within the first year of a baby's life as well as the discussions held on parent evenings are clear indications that parents want to have a good look at their child developing. At the beginning of a baby's life they are particularly motivated and interested in furthering their child *correctly*.

As they are not yet *experts* in their parental role they should be provided with qualified advice referring to the development of the child in its entirety.

In baby swimming the course instructor looks after, guides and teaches not only the babies but their parents as well. With the many expectations that the parents have and their experiences up to now the main learning aims are:

◆ to hold the baby securely in the water – to enhance its wellbeing in water;
◆ to accompany the child in its development and motivate it through play and movement exercises;
◆ to strike up contact with others, to get to know songs and ideas for playing.

The course instructor gives the answer to all 'how?' questions here.

Adults have differing attitudes to water. Some take part in water sports, others are holiday swimmers and others again are hesitant in the water.

In a swimming pool parents can experience how their baby feels quite free in the water; they can learn to really enjoy moving around and playing with the child, develop a feeling for sensory experiences and for the necessary body contact to the child in water; they both consciously adapt their movement behaviour to the child (and not the other way round!) and implement their function of example; both parties can really get to know each other through body language.

The almost nakedness in the water intensifies the relationship through body contact.

In game situations parents learn just how much space and motivation their child wants from them, how to deal with their child's curiosity, creativity and spontaneity as well as how to convey safety, calmness and trust to it in unexpected situations.

3.2 Course Instructors as Teachers and Sensitive Parental Advisors

A course instructor must be aware of the variety of expectations that parents have. Within a course they not only want to be catered for as regards course content; they also want to be looked after while retaining their own freedom of activity. The course instructor is essentially obliged to fulfil the following tasks:

◆ pre-course information about organisational prerequirements and methods used

◆ explain and convey lesson contents

◆ gripping and diving techniques must be explained as regards their advantages and disadvantages. Parents should also learn about the physical properties of water and how to use them. Learning songs and certain games means the parental repertoire is extended and singing in a group is easier for the not so keen singers. Hints and game ideas for all areas of a child's development help the parents to gradually get a feeling for their child's abilities.

◆ observe the group and individual parent-child couples and correct as a whole or individually.

◆ be able to sense the atmosphere

◆ through conversations held with other adults, parents can discuss their problems and insecurities; this enhances the development of trust, feelings of resonsibility and a willingness to help. If the participants are happy together in a group over several months a strong communal spirit reigns. It is important though to be also tolerant of other opinions.

◆ advise the parents on specific questions within their (instructor's) area of competence.

In order to bring about a qualitative improvement parents should be informed on and have a complete understanding of furthering development. Apart from grip and diving techniques, alternative ideas and playful activities, it is particularly important that the instructor conveys knowledge about factors which can influence movement, i.e. clearly explain to the parents the various possibilities of action for health-oriented behaviour. The instructor should give concrete examples of and show variations in holding, carrying and transporting a baby

Baby Swimming

From the aspect of method and contents, the body contact between mother and child should be taken into more consideration than up to now. Lessons which were previously centred around the child should now include more work with a baby's 'trust' persons. A fundamental objective of this swimming together in water, an objective which can be reached by all means, is to let parents consciously feel and perceive (through specific hints) the effects of this body contact between mother and child.

The concept behind training and further education courses enabling swimming instructors to give baby swimming lessons should not only focus on water-specific behaviour but also on the general psychological and pedagogical parent-child behaviour. Along with specific knowledge more importance should be attached to looking at what influences and promotes development accompanied by specific knowledge.

In order to promote development with the main focus lying on motor activity one requires knowledge of development stages and the different ways of initiating movement by means of appropriate handling; the instructor must use this knowledge and bring it into harmony with the parents' ideas on how the child becomes independent. By deliberately waiting and challenging the child's movement performance in lessons or everyday life the baby is given enough 'room' *to manage things by itself.*

By sorting the different states of development and dividing up the groups according to age, the course instructor can offer more appropriate activities in his lessons thus furthering the development of specific individual motor skills.

4 Baby Swimming

4.1 A Historical Perspective and Research Findings

According to sagas, murals and reports from ancient times, children in tribes who lived near water were used to water from very early on. Water meant nourishment and a quality of life for those living on islands. The Greeks saw swimming at a young age as a sign of education, the Celts and the Teutons used cold water for immersing babies so as to get them hardy. Not much is known about children´s confrontation with water in the Middle Ages.

In 1897 MUMFORD described babies' movements as *swimming movements*. He noticed that babies in prone position (under dry conditions) conducted rhythmical, outward and backward stretching and bending movements with their arms and legs. Scientific examinations of babies in water were carried out by WATSON as early as 1919. He noticed *uncoordinated mass movements* in supine position. In 1939 McGRAW reported of *reflex swimming movements* in the first four months of life and a reflex blocking of breathing when babies went under water.

These *swimming movements* are described as being a coordinated (slight) forward movement triggered off through the lateral flexion of the trunk and the rhythmical movement of the arms and legs. MAYERHOFER (1952) and PEIPER (1961) referred to the inherent *swimming reflex* as a baby's *phylogenetic*[16] memory of its life before birth. They were able to identify cross-coordinated swimming movements up until the fifth month.

BAUERMEISTER (1984) and BRESGES/DIEM (1983) see babies' swimming movements as *instinct movements*, which can be stimulated as preparation for unaided swimming in the future from the third year of life. WIELKI/HOUBEN (1983) confirmed evidence of reflex swimming movements up to the fifth month which were replaced by uncoordinated patterns of movement; these in turn changed to become voluntary swimming movements from the eleventh month on.

---

[16] Referring to family history.

In the course of the research on intelligence and learning in the 1970s the trend headed toward producing empirical evidence on the various possibilites of furthering a child from an early age, particularly in the field of remedial education (KOCH 1969; EGGERT/SCHUCK 1972; SCHILLING 1973 among others). The expression 'early stimulation' established a name for itself.

Worth mentioning here is the scientific analysis by DIEM/LEHR/ OLBRICH/UNDEUTSCH (1980) on the effects of early stimulation in water on the development of a child's personality in the third and fourth year of its life. 183 'water babies' were tested with the following result: what distinguished baby swimmers from their non-swimming peers was their better situative adaptiveness, higher level of self-confidence and independence (ibid. 15).

Around about the same time swimming schools and swimming courses came into being (BAUERMEISTER among others). The ensuing extension and modernising measures on swimming pools to become so-called 'fun and adventure pools' with a warm water pool for babies caused a rise in popularity of swimming in general and in the maelstrom to an outspread of baby swimming in Germany. Similarly, parents became more interested in and made use of courses for babies and toddlers within the framework of family leisure planning in the 90s.

Of the few statistical examinations on the effects of baby swimming on child development, PLIMPTON's examination in 1986 stands out. The influence of movements on motor development and a child's interactive behaviour in water and dry conditions was examined over a period of seven months on babies aged 9.5 months on average.

Judges observed children's movement behaviour in the following areas: moving, smiling, making sounds, touching, grasping and crying. Clear trends were visible in the study: children who as well as being in normal parent-child groups also took part in water programmes proved to have a larger repertoire of movements and a more positive emotional behaviour.

MOULIN (1997) examined the development of children's independence according to the extent of water activity on babies aged 9-30 months over a period of two years. The tests were carried out four times at 6 month intervals in each case, by way of a questionnaire, systematic lesson observations, an interaction analysis as well as testing processes for development diagnosis. At the age of 30 months significant differences as regards motor skills, psychosocial stability and performance capacity were established between the group of 'swimmers' and the test group. The results of the

interaction analysis were also clearly in favour of the 'water babies': the swimmers' communicative and exploring playing behaviour was more intensive than that of the other group.

NUMMINEN/SÄÄKSLATHI (1998) carried out a study to assess water stimulus on the development of motor skills on babies aged 5-6 months over a period of nine months. For this study the parents kept a diary which had been compiled on the basis of motor characteristics of development diagnosis. According to the result early swimming promotes a child's abilities to grasp, stretch, prop his arms up as well as to sit.

In addition to this the author has conducted studies at the German Sports Univerity on the following themes:
◆ *The IDOSI study* (Infectious Disease of Swimming Infants) (1997), in which the frequency of illness in those babies who were stimulated

by water in the first year of life was compared with those who weren't. *The result:* babies who take part in swimming aren't ill more often than their peers. It became clear that breastfeeding in the lying phase served to protect babies from illness and that in general illnesses became more frequent due to teething, weaning and independent movement around.

◆ *The WaGuM study* (Wasserguss method = water-pouring method) (1998). Assuming the theory of perceptive learning a new technique for headfirst ducking (diving) was examined by way of the water-pouring test. In order to do this the baby was made familiar with the water gradually and its emotional eagerness to dive into the water was checked, before its face was briefly ducked in the water following a positive reaction. It was found out that a baby's willingness to duck can be assessed through this pouring method and that there are definite connections between a baby's form on that day, his reaction to the pouring test and the post-diving reaction.

◆ *The WaVeK Study* (Wasservertrautheit von Kleinkindern = toddlers' familiarity with water) (2000). This compared toddlers' self-confidence and their reactions to various water situations during a playground -like circuit in a shower room. Those children swimming from an early age proved to be decidedly more open-minded and comfortable around water in comparison to the other children.

◆ *The MUKi Study* (Motorische Untersuchung von Kindern im ersten Lebensjahr = examination of children's motor activity in the first year of life) (2000). This study looked at the effect of baby swimming on motor activity and also checked whether and to what extent a mother's attitude to her own body influences her baby's movement development. The results made it clear that swimming, particularly in the lying phase is beneficial to posture. There were indications at a later age of better motor performances evident in babies stimulated by water at an early age. A mother's positive attitude to body contact turned out to have a supporting influence on her child's motor skills.

4.2 Teaching Methods and Objectives

There are numerous methods for teaching baby swimming. They originally stem from diverse methodic approaches. These diversities are in turn a consequence of the different objectives of those running the course and depend on spatial, organisatory and internal factors. The course instructor's qualifications, the example he sets and his own personal style of teaching are the remaining factors. To what extent clear, oriented teaching concepts exist or are adhered to is another matter. Trends and international influences go down well.

In practice there is a broad, variable range of possibilities for laying out a course: set courses and course times where one can pick a day that suits, baby groups which are homogeneous or heterogeneous from an age aspect, objective-oriented ideas and open playing opportunities, one-to-one or group lessons. Courses are run or supervised according to the teaching methods.

If one were to systemise the most important methodic concepts (whereby certain common factors are to be seen), they can be classified according to prime objectives and course contents as following:

◆ *Sport pedagogic* lesson concepts see learning and performance motives as a priority as regards work content. These include:
  ◆ Programmes for getting familiar with water, specifically carried out in preparation for swimming lessons.
  ◆ Conveyance of 'save yourself' techniques , to reduce the rate of child drowning by guiding the child towards an independent ability to survive from an early age.
  Such offers support a child's sport socialisation into the community at an early age, as well as encouraging and promoting the child in movement and coordination; parents who are interested in or active in sport can be built into the lesson as a good example.
◆ *Psychological* concepts have the main aim of play and having fun or overcoming fear. The lessons are structured on personal experience. Water, a primary element, should be experienced without fear, water inhibitions are to be broken and negative experiences with water are to be dealt with. Water takes on a uniting role, enabling parents to share intensive body contact with their child and strike up contact with others in the group while experiencing and playing together.
◆ *Medically* based concepts: health promotion or health therapy are priority here. From the preventive aspect one orientates oneself in general to a child's entire normal development. From a rehabilitative aspect one devotes particular attention to the improvement of certain diagnosed ability deficits. Hydrotherapy involves the conscious implementing of water's physical properties. Well known in physiotherapy for the rehabilitation of handicapped in water are in particular the Halliwick methods according to McMILLAN (1976) (cf. SCHMIDT-HANSBERG 1981) and the buoyancy therapy according to KRAFFT (1961,1974), the contents of which are partially used for babies.

4.3 The Concept of Early Stimulation

Early stimulation of motor activity

Through early motor stimulation the baby is pushed and invited to develop further. This type of stimulation involves motivating, triggering off, initiating or challenging the child to some active movement. The movement can be triggered off by different sense stimuli although the effectiveness of this stimulus depends on the organism's state. By digesting these perceptions its discovery instinct and desire to move is set off, its confidence in its own movements boosted. As well as this, it learns how to adapt to its environment through these movement experiences.

The important thing for the child is not its ability "to sit or stand from an early age, but rather that it can get into an upright position through its own initiative and the way it does this" (DIEM 1967, 19).

Furthering development with the main focus on motor skills

"Let us still remain with the comparison between the organism and a picture moving from its blueprint stage while coming into being. The stages of development are incomplete, a number of various directions are still possible, which are then eliminated in the mature picture, i.e. the completion in a chosen direction. In just the same way a growing shoot on its path of development is incomplete and thus threatens to take on other possible forms (....)".

(PORTMANN 1972, 165)

This also means that moments depending on maturity as well as on learning and practice both play a part in the development process. Thus a child should be given the opportunities to gather experience and reproduce its behaviour either innerly or by actually carrying it out. This holds for a baby's passive and active experiences of movement through transfer effects and practice. The objective of furthering is to develop a baby's movement ability and activity as well as to unfold its own activity while discovering and playing.

Baby Swimming

At the beginning it needs its parents' help and care due to its biologically-determined helplessness, but the way it is helped determines its own activity as well as its natural development both of which it itself must *initiate*.

The aim is to arouse the child's interest and – with patience and endurance – to reinforce the way it comes to terms with its environment. The child is enabled to think and act independently. Its learning experiences help give it more self-control and independence.

Moving and perceiving are mutually dependent. This becomes more evident with growing sight. That is when the baby becomes increasingly interested in objects and facial expression, which in turn sets off a stimulus to move. As the process goes on both the medium water along with its special physical properties are used for stimulating motor activity in the entire body.

Throughout the exercises in the water – carried out corresponding to a child's development stage and in a variety of forms – sensory stimuli which consequently spur on the baby's senses are deliberately integrated, e.g. flowing water over the palms of his hands or the soles of his feet, which in turn motivates the child to feel its body itself. Information is taken in and is suitably processed in the central nervous system. "*Every improvement of information through perception sensitisation leads to an improvement in the quality of action and vice versa -every voluntary motor action and every adaptive motor reaction results in better perception and in turn a higher level of organisation and integration of neurological regulatory circuit*" (KIPHARD 1981, 76). Stimulation is particularly fruitful when the activities meet with a positive response and arouse the desire for new challenges both in the children and in the parents. The child's level and sequence of development determines what type of stimulation is selected and its efficiency. The type of stimulation chosen is offered in a playful form, how it's accepted and translated into action is observed quantitively and qualitatively and corrected where necessary.

A child perceives sensory and motor promotion in the following areas; each can be separately stimulated but only form a unit altogether (cf. KIPHARD 1981). The exercises are directed in such a way as to improve the following abilities:

◆ Total body control in the form of support, positioning, tensing, compensation of movements e.g. after a change of position.
◆ Hand and finger skills in grasping and letting go.
◆ *Oral skills* in the form of chewing, sucking, licking, blowing, sound imitation and babbling motivation.
◆ *Eye skills* to focus on an object or pursue a target.
◆ Optical perception in the form of colours, shapes, sizes, amounts as well as of its own body.
◆ Acoustic perception through non-verbal differentiation and localisation of sounds as well as the development in word comprehension through verbal repetition.
◆ Kinesthetic perception through turning and rocking movements, to improve the sensation of position and muscle and adapt muscle tone according to the particular movement.
◆ Tactile perception through mechanical or thermal skin stimulation.
◆ Smelling perception through various smell stimuli.
◆ Tasting perception of many different things offered.

How effective and successful these stimulations are depends mainly on the suitable methodic selection of stimulus on the sense organs, under favourable general conditions as regards room, time, personnel and temperature.

Through early and varied motivation the child develops its thinking and recognising processes while handling and playing with objects, with a partner or in a group. It develops its movement activities, improves its abilities, discovers its needs and experiences itself. By taking a good look at its surroundings it makes use of its personal natural abilities at its own rhythm. The ability to deal with its environment boosts its self-confidence. It is important that parents, guardians, teachers etc. are fundamentally aware that surrounding factors have a sustained effect on movement development and pay attention to this. The diverse offers of our spectrum of action can have both an impeding and furthering effect on development when all biogenetic factors and individual differences are not taken into consideration. Increasing these offers is not necessarily beneficial to development. The length and intensivity of stimulus – regardless of the latest trends – must be carried out in line with the state of development and be in the correct dosage.

Through early motor stimulation of babies it is possible to pick up and work on movement weaknesses which occur during the pregnancy/at the birth or other factors as soon as they start to appear. It is assumed that patterns of movement are not yet cerebrally stable when a person is in the state of 'physiological prematurity', i.e. a baby's development is not completed before the end of the first year; thus its movements can be therapeutically influenced.

The orientated furthering of coordinative abilities and elementary forms of movement can never occur too early, as the later coordination abilities are determined by the amount of practice over the first 22 months (cf. McGRAW 1975). The period of time between the sixth week and sixth month is seen as a baby's sensitive phase, a learning phase during which the organism should get motivation, ideas and opportunities to practise. It's a period in which a baby perceives more consciously but is not yet able to stimulate itself enough yet. It has been proved that daily half-hour movement exercises cause development to be 2-4 months ahead, i.e. it is possible to modify motor development through learning processes. The dexterity which is achieved through early stimulation can be seen not only in particular abilities but through motor skills as a whole.

Early stimulation through baby swimming

The teaching concept of *early stimulation* through *baby swimming* assumes that

◆ the chronologically fixed courses are run and taken part in *regularly* once a week for 30-45 minutes;

◆ teaching takes place in *groups*, in which no more than eight to ten parent-child couples have to be catered for;

◆ the groups are formed according to the babies' *age and state of development;*

◆ the (full-term) babies begin with swimming at an *age of 2-3 months;*

◆ the lesson has a *well-ordered structure of content* which apart from teaching gripping and diving techniques also gives ideas and motivation *for arm and leg movement* and sensitises *perception;*

◆ the course content is given by *qualified* instructors and applied specifically for early stimulation of movement and perception;

◆ in the first year swimming aids attached to the body are *not* used for long as this would restrict a baby's freedom of movement;

◆ the water is consciously used as environmental stimulus, for the stimulation of instinctive reflex swimming movements and of respiratory reaction, for getting the babies familiar with the medium of water, for *assessing their willingness to dive* under and where possible for diving itself;

◆ toys are *not* lying around in the water as *constant stimulus,* but only introduced after a long period of active working with the water.

4.4 Success Anticipated and the Results

Baby swimming is not to be reduced to a sheer stimulus-reaction mechanism but is rather to be seen as an interactive occurrence between child and parent, or alternatively as interaction between course instructor, parent and child.

The range and diversity of child development conditions implies that baby swimming can only have a promotive effect from a *context-specific*[17] aspect. Teaching baby swimming *in its entirety* implies promoting both motor skill and perception, offering mental motivation and having creative playing situations, and creating common emotional parent-child experiences where movement is enjoyed. In the process certain surmounting situations arise which are necessary for learning and experiencing something new. Last but not least working together calls for discipline, to the effect that the individuality of other types of behaviour and child-rearing approaches are tolerated.

The expectations can be defined as follows:
◆ Particularly when a baby is very young and not able to get from A to B by itself baby swimming is beneficial to its structure of posture; when it's a bit older movement coordination becomes more flowing.
◆ The everyday handling of the child, depending on parental rearing methods also has a considerable effect on development; frequently setting down a child or taking it by the hand when learning to walk impede the baby's abilities to attempt things itself. Naked kicking, experimenting with its own body turns out to be much more conducive to development; the more space the child is given for discovering by itself the more beneficial this is to its motor development. Baby swimming is no exception. Parental observing attention and kind words must also be present.

---

[17] The child's surrounding social connections (i.e. living and rearing conditions).

◆ For a baby, body contact with its parents is a very influential factor in motor development from the aspect of movement experience. Interactive, movement-intensive forms of play have a stimulating effect as the baby is required to keep control over its body in the process.

The pedagogic-psychological care of parents and babies helps in getting to know the child and its natural physical abilities and observing them individually.

Regularity

When one has made the decision to take part in baby swimming, this is the most difficult part. Chances of successful motor development rise and then fall again without regular participation, i.e. at least once a week. In other words: success depends to a large extent on one's willingness to take part regularly, i.e. weekly. Sporadic appearance, i.e. every two weeks, significantly reduces the sustained effects of baby swimming.

The advantages to be gained from taking part in baby swimming are confirmed by the results of the MUKi (motor examination of children in their first year) study. This was carried out between 1997-1999 in Cologne with 215 babies in total and through this study it was possible to assess the effects of baby swimming on motor skills as well as observe the influence of a mother's own body concept. It turned out that baby swimming, through body and movement stimulation coordinates sensory and motor skills. The children had a better sitting posture at various growing stages.

One could notice an improvement in body coordination in the form of more sensitive balance reactions in creeping, walking and crouching movements, leg differentiation when turning around as well as finely tuned balance reactions. This is due to the fact that through baby swimming the back muscles in particular are strengthened and the organ of balance is stimulated.

The great differences and the connections established between the child's state of development and the parental forms of interaction confirm and explain that parents stimulate their baby with *differing movement intensity.*

This clearly shows that there are *limits* as regards both the motor stimulation of the baby and the pedagogic care of the child. How content the mother was with her body as a baby and her positive attitude to body contact at a later toddler age influence child motor development positively. This also includes the mother's attitude to her own sportiness and her satisfaction with her personal appearance.

III The Practical Application Of Baby Swimming

5 Planning and Organisation of a Course

Institutions offering baby swimming courses have different possibilities available of carrying out such a course. The first thing to do is to awaken and reach people's interests by advertising in club course programmes, adult education centre leaflets etc. or through a newspaper advertisement with follow-up advice and information either over the telephone or by post. When all the organisational preparations are more or less complete i.e. as regards participants, venue and time, it's time for the detailed work to begin.

5.1 Planning and Conceiving a Course

Generally speaking the courses can run all year round, parents without schoolgoing children don't tend to take holiday breaks in the main season. The course instructor determines the style of lesson and this is explained in a short leaflet for the general public. Both an *open* course concept – a meeting of families where the non-central teaching person is there to supervise and give the parents advice or information on request – and a *closed* course concept – with a centralised teacher, a structured lesson and small groups divided up according to age – are possible. A course of 10-15 units (with no holiday interruptions) has proved to be worthwhile. 9.00-12.00 in the morning or 3.00 pm-6.00 pm in the afternoons are the most suitable hours available as babies are normally active during these times. The younger a baby is the more irregular its sleeping and awake patterns are. The older a baby is the more used it is to a particular daily routine. When enrolling for the course the parents should make sure from then on to consciously fit swimming into their daily routine and forget about other activities or efforts on those days so as not to overtax or overstress the child.

The group should consist of about eight babies with their mothers/fathers/trust persons. A good idea is for both parents to accompany the child at the beginning so that both are informed about the run of events. During a 'making strange' phase however, it is wise to have only one person present, as during this emotionally unstable phase it is often easier to calm down a child when it can concentrate on one person.

Groups should be divided up according to age and perhaps according to 'newcomers' and 're-enrollers', i.e. one should ask about previous knowledge when the participants are enrolling.

The water should be 1.3 m deep at the most (i.e. chest height) and be 32-33° for baby swimming. Open air swimming can generally not be recommended yet because of the low surrounding temperatures outdoors. For reasons to do with strict water quality control one should choose indoor swimming pools; as a surrounding temperature of 34-35° is a further argument.

30-45 min is a suitable length of time to stay in the water. At the beginning of the course, when the full 45 minutes are not completely used up in the water, massage tips and circles for play or discussion can be built in.

5.2 Parent Evenings and Preparation in the Pool

The following themes should be dealt with on a parent evening:

◆ who to consult with organisatory enquiries (enrolling, cancelling and re-enrolling), course instructor's role (qualification, amount of experience);

◆ swimming pool venue (how to get there, availability of parking spaces, spaces for 'parking' prams, changing rooms, showering and baby-changing facilities, pool description, depth of water);

◆ structure and aim of courses (this course, follow-up courses, size of groups, children's age difference, person accompanying the child (mother and/or father), brothers or sisters, working parallel to development, promotion of posture, movement and perception, social contacts, parent-child experience);

◆ lesson structure and content (lesson in 4 phases: gymnastic and movement exercises, grip and diving techniques, ideas for play, songs and opportunities to relax).

◆ parents (ask about previous experience, explain preparation possibilities in the bath) health benefits of swimming together;
◆ clarify hygienic and security measures (swimming gear, showering);
◆ prerequirements for the child (premature or full-term, state of health, doctor's certificate).

The parents are required to provide a certificate from a (paediatric) doctor so as to confirm that the child is fit enough for physical load and does not have any contagious diseases, (e.g. diarrhoea, conjunctivitis, flu). There are very few medical reasons for baby swimming to be forbidden. These include very serious heart defects, lung malformations or open wounds.

Swimming clothing:
◆ One should always bring several hand towels to the lesson. One is used for changing the baby on to protect it from germs, another for drying the baby.
◆ A baby's swimsuit consists of either 'trainers' with microfibre lining, or towelled briefs with firm, elasticated legs.
◆ It's not always avoidable (although because of the water pressure it does actually happen seldom) that a baby urinates in the water. It's more likely to happen after swimming. For this reason it is advisable to wrap a baby in a towel directly after showering and then put its nappy on.

Bathing at home - not just skincare

As soon as the belly button has healed a baby can be bathed in suitably warm water (without adding anything to it), starting off with five minutes and then increasing up to fifteen minutes. As long as the baby is still small the wash basin or a baby bath/tub can be used for this. In order for it not to be just a washing process, but rather a lively one of letting out steam with kicking and splashing, playing, cuddling and relaxing, it can become a real experience for mother, father and child in a big bath together. A wet (not overflooded) bathroom should not be a hindering factor. One can practise the first handling, the baby's movements are motivated and by being swayed he can later relax, lying weightlessly. Bathing in the evening has generally proved to be worthwhile through its positive effects on a baby's sleeping habits. It is amazing to think that in our culture parents often give their children a bath once a week. In southern cultures daily bathing rituals are very common.

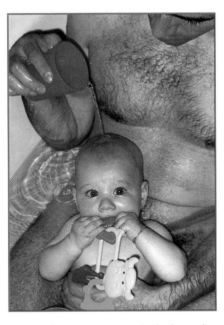

As long as there are no skin-related objections to it we see no arguments against more frequent bathing. On the contrary, a baby gets the opportunity *to let off steam*. It can enjoy the physical contact to its parents, particularly to the father, as – due to breastfeeding – the mother already provides the child with regular, intensive body closeness..

A very young baby is held upright or in supine position with its head leaning on a parent's shoulder (see Chapter 6.2.2 S) for support. In this position one can stroke, massage and cover its body with water so as to also prevent it from cooling. When it has got used to the wet environment after a few minutes one activates its circulation with up and down bouncing movements of its arms; forward and backward sweeping movements and sidewards swinging movements in the vertical 'sandwich grip'. When the baby is lying on its back on one's knees it is possible to watch it and moisten it. Or one places it into prone position on one's shins holding it with one hand and sprinkling its back or pouring water on its head with the other so as to encourage it to move its arms and legs. With these little drops and slight water showers the baby gets familiar with the technique for holding its breath. A little beaker helps to regulate the amount of water used. One begins with a small veil of water and gradually accustoms the baby to having water flowing over its face for about two seconds, while speaking quiet words of encouragement. This procedure should be repeated about three times. If the baby clearly puts up a fight then one should stop.

Lying in prone posion on both hands (chalice and basket grips), (see chapter 6.2.2 D and E), or in supine position (towing grip) (see chapter 6.2.2 U), the baby can be pushed and pulled through the water far enough for its feet to feel the end of the bath, thus encouraging it to make kicking movements.

Whatever objects are available can be used for playing with, such as facecloths and sponges, colourful beakers etc. The child becomes attentive and looks around, it can feel something, grasp it and put it in its mouth. In this way it gradually develops skills by grasping on its own and its (playing) interests are aroused.

Parents should preferably make use of the following forms of play for getting their baby accustomed to water:
◆ stroking and sprinkling its head with water;
◆ pouring water over its head or showering it (see, feel, sense);
◆ making waves roll against the body;
◆ finger games and hands splashing in the water;
◆ pulling and pushing the baby through the water.

Bathing in the water for around 15 minutes should always be carefully aimed at the baby and its mother or father feeling comfortable in the water together and being able to relax. Without any rush, with quiet words and changing positions and grips (heart-to-heart, relax, head bowl, chalice, basket) as well as by petting the child's body, the time spent in the water becomes a very pleasant experience and can also be introduced as a going to bed ritual or for movement compensation.

5.3 Some Practical Points of Advice

When standing in shallow water (about 1.3 m) there is a danger of a parent's body cooling when its skin is wet, especially around the shoulder area. For this reason parents – and babies – should always assume a vertical position where the water is at shoulder height. One must pay attention to this during the lesson. If the baby is lying on its back or its stomach, one must ensure and point out that those parts of the body which are not in the water are constantly moistened and covered. This is particularly the case for play situations on the steps going into the water or on the swimming mats.

The maximal duration in the water for a baby fundamentally depends on the water temperature, but also on the frequency of swimming lessons (how accustomed the child is), age, pleasure derived from movements and what form the baby's in that day; these points must always be considered.

For example, if a baby starts to get cold due to insufficient sleep, a recent illness, teething or hunger, then this is a clear sign, and it is a good idea not to continue that day. In order to test if a child is cold, one can check the blood supply of its skin by pressing one's index finger against its lower arm (finger pressure test). If this bright mark remains for a good while then the blood supply of the skin has dropped significantly and one should come out of the water and warm its body up.

For those parts of the body far away from the heart, such as the hands and the feet, this can be most easily recognised through paleness of the skin as the hair follicle structure is not yet developed. When a baby is cold, it doesn't have goose pimples or rattling teeth – this sets in at a later age – but rather its posture is huddled, it has a staring facial expression, pale skin and it isn't enjoying the water as much.

However, many babies' teeth can be seen rattling even at the beginning of the lesson; this is frequently due to excitement.

After about twenty minutes, babies' concentration and movement intensity dwindles noticeably, so that one should then finish off the lesson nice and calmly.

5.4 Hygiene and Prevention of Illness

Swimming keeps one's body fit and healthy. So as to avoid accidentally injuring oneself or becoming ill as a result of improper behaviour some important basic rules must be obeyed. In the case of baby swimming this comes under the parents' responsibility.

Needless to say only babies who are feeling well may take part in swimming. Whether or not one goes to swimming with 'the sniffles' is a matter of discretion which the parents must decide. In this case it is advisable to have tissues ready at the side of the pool so as to be able to regularly clean its nose as the combination of hot and cold air encourages their noses to run.

Diving underwater should be avoided here. Every one in the pool should either tie their hair up or (depending on regulations) wear a swimming cap rather than having loose hair swimming around in the water as this is unpleasant particularly near one's hands and mouth.

I have already dealt with the issue of water being at shoulder-level and wetting those parts of the body out of the water so as to avoid cooling, in chapter 5.3.

As well as the hygienic pre-requirements set by the swimming institute all course participants must also ensure that they themselves are not a source of germs. This implies a precept on cleanliness which begins with a shower (*without* swimsuit) before entering the pool. The desire to pass water normally sets in immediately after leaving the water, it is advisable to wrap the child up directly after showering and put on its nappy as soon as possible.

After swimming, all wet clothes should be taken off. A hand towel from home should be lying at the side of the pool to put around the child before showering or changing. Showering afterwards is another act of hygiene. A rubber tube pulled over the shower nozzle cuts down the noise and the speed the water comes out at. This simple construction also means there are no sudden splashes, which can frighten a young baby and lessen his enjoyment of showering.

The shower before entering the pool should be lukewarm whereas all participants should have a warm shower afterwards so as to warm up again more quickly.

As a preventative measure, a baby should be dressed and undressed according to an 'onion system' (i.e. layer by layer) so that the child's body can adapt to changes of temperature step by step. Babies sweat or get cold so quickly because their thermal regulation systems are not fully developed. By rolling the baby to each side, any water which has managed to get into its ears can run out.

Babies are changed either under a wall heater or on the floor on a thick insulating mat and ideally be dressed into a bodysuit and perhaps tights. The remain clothing can be left off until one leaves the building so as to avoid overheating. Warm tea, a breastfeed and massaging in lotion all help to warm up the baby. Before leaving the building one should use a hairdryer to dry the baby's hair and inside his ears, and put his hat on to prevent it catching a draught.

5.5 First Aid and the Duties of Care and Responsibility to the Child

Preventative measures are necessary in a swimming pool in order to be able to react quickly in the case of accidents and injuries. For a course instructor to be able to provide fast and proper aid, he must be familiar with first aid measures.

First aid courses specifically for babies are run by charity health organisations and in children's hospitals. Before beginning a baby swimming course one must ensure that the pool area has no dangerous spots, the first-aid cupboard is full and that the telephone is in working order. One must be aware of the rescue apparatus available, where the emergency exits are and which hospital is reponsible for that area and can be contacted in an emergency.[x]

Statistically seen, accidents in swimming pools occur seldom. They're normally a result of running (danger of slipping), insufficient attentiveness and supervision, the incorrect use of equipment or existing organic weaknesses a person may have. A young baby, limited in its activity, is less liable to have an accident than an older baby who can move round. The typical accidents with babies are due to suffocation (when something has gone down the wrong way), poisoning or corrosion (from acids), scalding and burning or from a fall.

What can happen in baby swimming and how the course instructor can combat these dangers through an explanatory discussion with the parents is listed as follows:

---

[x] A course instructor must have so-called 'limited' rescue abilities for the beginners' pool (depth up to 1.35 m). This includes (in Germany) having the bronze swimming badge (proof of one's ability to swim over 10 metres and dive 1.35 m, to swim 200 m in 7 minutes at the most as well as knowing the swimming rules) and being able to give first aid. These tests are carried out by swimming and lifesaving associations and the water watch division of the (German) Red Cross.

◆ Falls can occur during a nappy change, by slipping on the floor at the pool edge, outside the pool or on the wide steps during jumping-in situations. By changing the baby on the floor on soft mats, wearing flip-flops and making jumping-in situations safe with the use of soft mats these dangers can be prevented. Shoulder, head, elbow or wrist injuries such as grazing, straining or cuts can occur in jumping-in situations when the parents keep an unsuitable safe distance to their child resulting in it landing directly on them instead of in the water. Water's resistance prevents them from drifting back again. The danger with the first jumping attempts – falling into the water from a sitting position at the edge of the pool – is that the baby scrapes its head or back off the edge when it doesn't lean forward enough. For a safe performance of this see chapter 6.2.2 (W). Hand, elbow or shoulder injuries can occur when the child is held the wrong way, e.g. when the parents, instead of holding its trunk place their hands out; then when it falls they push it back up again with their hands to prevent it from going under. This is why a course instructor must explain the different grips in detail and correct them during the exercises.

◆ Poisoning can occur when a child drinks large amounts of chlorinised water, shower gel/shampoos or foot disinfectant. By supporting the child's head securely above water and keeping an eye on it (in the shower rooms) this can be avoided. Pool water is of drinking water standard, i.e. a drink of it alone does not cause poisoning (water intoxication).

◆ Bouts of suffocation can occur when small parts go down the wrong way. They enter the airways and partially or completely block the lungs. Therefore both course instructor and parents must always examine playing material. To avoid a sudden fall or a tumble into the water, where the baby's head is under water for a while and it gasps for air and starts to panic, an accompanying adult must be within *reaching distance* at all times. Babies who are already able to move about have to be made familiar with the safety rules and signals, i.e. they are to sit on the steps or the edge and are not allowed to crawl or run around until a parent is in the water and gives a signal to jump. Danger is lurking when parents aren't watching for a second and the children swim out of their parents' reach with a swimming ring or water wings. A comment here: older brothers or sisters can only be integrated into the course to a limited extent for this reason; a second accompanying person is recommended. Because of the lack of supervision one cannot allow the older child to swim around on its own with swimming aids or stand waiting at the edge of the pool. Experience shows that parents are inclined to widen their distance to the child when swimming aids are used, as they assume their child to be in safety.

When something has been swallowed the wrong way (aspiration) e.g. small hard pieces, it is necessary to get the child to cough. In the case of solid pieces one lays the child stomach-down on one's thighs and slaps it on the back 3-4 times; or the baby is lying flat and is being held at the shoulder and hip joints and is then suddenly turned almost upside-down, back and forth, giving the object the opportunity to move up out of the baby's airways. If the child swallows water the wrong way, coughing and sneezing set in on reflex thus transporting the water back out again. By holding the child close to one's body, with eye contact, calming words of affection and by supporting the back of its head as well as tapping its back his condition is usually brought back to normal quickly.

Drowning is when a baby loses consciousness; if it stops breathing or it comes to cardiovascular standstill, medical assistance must be sought immediately. When a baby is still breathing it must be immediately laid down on the floor in a lateral position wrapped up warm and dry and comforted.

After brief observation (nostril or chest movements) and attempts at stimulation (talking to it, blowing, shaking) a child is found to be not breathing, one must clear the baby's mouth and immediately begin with artificial breathing, i.e. by completely covering both the baby's nose and mouth with one's own mouth and then breathing *four times*. After this its pulse rate is measured for about five seconds. If breathing does not begin again on its own after the initial breathing procedure but one can feel pulse, one must continue with artificial breathing *at a rate of 40 times a minute i.e. every 1.5 seconds* until the doctor arrives or the baby begins to breathe again (check pulse once a minute). To do this one tilts the head back slightly (not as far as with an adult) and holds the top of the skull with one hand, the other hand holds the chin with two fingers. One should breathe an amount of air suitable for the *size of the mouth* so as to avoid too much air coming into the lungs or the stomach.

When neither breathing nor pulse is evident then the heart has stopped beating. In this case artificial breathing must be carried out in sequence with cardiac massage on a hard surface. To find the right place to press, one lays one's index finger down on an imaginary line of connection between the nipples, the middle and ringer beside it and then lifts the index finger again; with two fingers the breastbone is pushed down by about *1.5-2 cm fifteen times* in close succession. There should be two compressions per second (approx. 100 presses per minute). *The working cycle of three breathing processes in alternation with fifteen cardiac massages* is to be continued until an ambulance arrives. If the heart begins to beat again, i.e. one can feel pulse rate, then only breathing should be continued.

Comment: It's generally hard to feel babies' pulse rate (hand, groin and throat arteries); recommended is putting on strong pressure on the upper arm which parents can practise while bathing.

One differentiates between 'wet' and 'dry' drowning. *Dry* drowning (10% of cases) is associated with an epiglottal cramp, i.e. because of the water which has entered the mouth or throat the epiglottis pushes itself in front of the trachea to prevent water from getting into the lungs. If the child is rescued in time artificial breathing is usually enough for successful resuscitation.

In the case of *wet* drowning a child is not found immediately. Through exhaustion the epiglottis relaxes again so that water gets into the lung and therefore into the blood circulation which can lead to life-threatening disruption of heart and kidney functions. A description is given of a successful resuscitation in freshwater even with children who were under water for 20 minutes or longer. Saltwater drowning is much more dangerous and a child can only survive with intensive medical treatment (cf. SEILER 1989).

The rule is: in the case of an accident the course instructor must act in a considered way, above all stay calm and not lose his head! The tasks must be divided up in order for the rescue chain to work, i.e. one person informs the rescue service (emergency telephone number with details on the accident (place,number and age of persons involved and type of accident)), another carries out the first aid procedures, another holds towels, mat etc. For the person doing the breathing it is very important that he takes deep breaths himself so as to prevent circulation problems. In order to find the right working rhythm for artificial breathing a 'training period' of 1-2 minutes is necessary.

The course instructor has the duty of responsibility for his group for the duration of the lesson, i.e. he informs the participants about potential danger, intervenes when this advice is not heeded, examines the pool area and ensures that the rules of the house and swimming regulations are obeyed. He is the first person to go into the water and the last to leave. From time to time it is necessary from a didactic point of view to explain/demonstrate/assess from outside the pool. Parents (or those 'trust persons' appointed to go swimming with the child) are responsible for their children. One must always be sure to find out whether there are non-swimmers or insecure swimmers among the parents. In this case one must grant specific supervision even if the water is shallow.

Legal responsibility for damages occurring to a person or his property during the lesson depends on the swimming institution in question. A course instructor is advised to clear up this issue with both the organisers and the participants or alternatively have an agreement in the course programme or the working contract. It goes without saying that every swimming instructor has liability insurance.

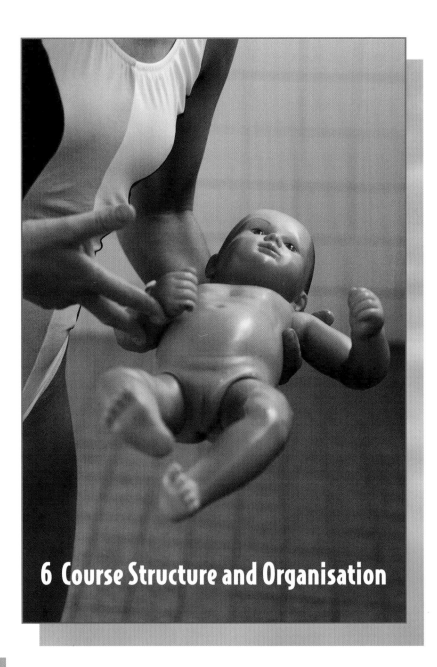

6 Course Structure and Organisation

6.1 Course Contents and Development

A course should be planned according to themes but without assigning learning steps to each particular lesson, as the babies, due to their age, their emotional instability and fluctuating ability to take in things depending on the form they're in that day, as well as their irregular attendance from time to time, have to be gradually accustomed to feeling comfortable in the water and moving around in it. They get integral motivation[18] which encourages them to show more interest in their surroundings. The acquiring of specific reactions can be initiated but not learned long-term (more of a getting used to at the beginning) as long as the baby is only able to take in and process a proportion of stimulus. Its memory capacity from a development psychology aspect is not fully matured.

There are four methodic didactic principles to be fundamentally heeded when organising a lesson: the lesson situation should promote the baby *integrally, healthily and at a level appropriate to his development*, and one should work in *harmony with the water*. Content method and duration progress must be structured from easy to difficult and simple to complex and then taught. One is there to technically encourage them in the lesson; one must see both the parents and the babies as learners.

When starting a course with beginners it is important not to have too much lesson content initially as this can overtax the participants. In order to bring the group together and to get all participants accustomed to the surroundings and the run of events it is necessary for the lesson to develop slowly with 'ice-breaking' activities and orientation games. The course instructor explains his ideas and their purpose. He must prepare himself for a variety of little problems which are to be dealt with: a baby's difficulties adapting, parents' unsureness and not much communication among the group members themselves before a certain routine has set in.

---

[18] Learning opportunities which aid personality development, i.e by encouraging both the physical motor abilities and social, emotional and intellectual abilities and by sensitising perception.

In the case of a second course, new lessons are still continually built on what the participants already know – adapted to the children's age and development phase. This includes repeating and varying content. In the case of long absences or holidays one must always plan in a renewed process of accustomization and repetition.

It has proved to be worthwhile to plan a lesson in such a way that the main themes of focus are picked out; one playing object is offered in each case for this purpose, to be used intensively in as many different ways as possible.

For babies of 3-6 months (beginners) the course sequence can have the following structure as regards subject matter:

Lesson and main theme focus:	Apparatus:
1st lesson: getting the group used to room, showers and pool as well as the first grip techniques: *heart to heart, confrontation, chalice*	coloured beakers
2nd lesson: getting-to know games and water-pouring method as well as grip techniques: *basket and relax*	doll and bowls
3rd lesson: water properties and effect of exercises as well as grip technique *leg tunnel*	sponges and washing line with wash pegs
4th lesson: getting used to water and diving methods as well as grip technique *arm cradle*	doll and plastic ducks
5th lesson: motivation to move about and grip technique *waiter's tray*	balls and bowls
6th lesson: parent-child interaction and grip technique *tête-à-tête*	egg-flips
7th lesson: child-child interaction and grip techniques *crane and armchair*	blowpipes
8th lesson: group activities and child-swop as well as grip technique *sandwich*	building blocks
9th lesson: possible relaxation activities and grip *technique water cradle*	swimming tubes and cloths with pegs as well as music
10th lesson: games of perception and grip technique *towing*	pot scrubbers and cosmetic sponges.

6.2 Constructing a Lesson, Lesson Content and Structuring a Lesson Creatively

The concept for each individual lesson is always structured into four phases and should go on for a maximum of 30/45 minutes[19] altogether.

◆ In the first phase (approx. 5 minutes) the child is *acclimatising* itself to the surroundings and to the water covering its body; its cardiovascular system is activated. The parent has close body contact to the baby and walks around the pool with it, massaging its body and petting its head with water. Gradually the parents intensify their movements while walking and hopping and then take their child out of this close skin and body contact position and place it in the 'confrontation' position so as to consciously have eye contact with it. During this exercise the baby's circulation is activated by raising and lowering its body.

◆ In the second phase (approx. 5 minutes) the baby's legs are stimulated through petting and shaking so that it can *consciously perceive* them. Through swaying, pushing and pulling movements in all directions against the water resistance the baby's sensations of skin, movement and position are sensitised and its orientative capacity is challenged at the same time. These new movements have the further aim of regulating muscle tone and making the joints more flexible.

◆ In the third phase (approx. 15 minutes) the child is increasingly encouraged *to move itself*. With the minimal amount of parental support required (hand under the chest) the baby is motivated to conduct movements by itself thanks to water splashes and currents, touching impulses on the soles of its feet or brief passive guidance of limb movement. With the help of the water-pouring test[20] the baby's willingness to dive under as well as its mouth-closing and non-breathing reflexes are assessed and, following a positive (emotional) behaviour on the baby's part, diving-under activities are carried out by the parents with the course instructor's assistance two to three times for one to two seconds. In a playful

form with the use of apparatus and playing materials where possible, the babies – again under guidance – are challenged to adapt their motor abilities with positioning reflexes and balancing reactions for flying, falling, grasping, supporting and turning movements. Those muscles responsible for posture and movement are strengthened during these endurance games.

◆ In the fourth phase (approx. 5 min) the child should be able or enabled *to relax* and satisfy its urge to play and discover. The child can pursue its interests without any instructions and should not be disturbed. Rocking cradle movements in supine position or a reclined sitting position calm down the baby's respiratory and cardiovascular systems, and the stimuli are gradually reduced toward the end of the lesson.

---

[19]   For babies up to six months 30 minutes, for babies over six months 45 minutes.
[20]   The water-pouring test assesses the baby's emotional attitude to water by familiarising it with it via flowing, pouring (not splashing) water.

Examples and ideas for lesson content and procedure:

1st lesson:
getting group used to room, showering rooms and pool
Materials: coloured beakers

Comment:

At the beginning of the lesson there should be a brief explanation of the lesson procedure to follow, what to do when the baby is unhappy in the water as well as advice on showering, body care and on dress. The instructor should demonstrate the different ways of showering, be it standing up, sitting or with the aid of a basin and the use of the tube; he must also lay down the points on hygienic behaviour in the swimming pool. During the first lesson the baby should receive a lot of body contact so that it feels comfortable in the strange surroundings.

Abbreviations:
PP = prone position
P = parents
B = baby
CI = course instructor
SP = supine position
ri = right, le =left
fw = forwards, bw = backwards

Phase/Duration	Objective
1 5 min	getting used to room
5 min	getting to know other participants
2 5 min	getting used to water
	pouring test with beaker
3 5 min	stimulate B's leg movement through touching
	B moves by itself
4 10 min	free play
	finishing up

Contents/method	Organisation	Teaching method
Heart-to-heart/Armchair: wandering through pool, "up and down" (until water is at shoulder height), varying grips. Form of play: "we're wandering, we're wandering from one place to another, and meet someone new (exchange names)" a) Embrace (eye contact, hands touching) b) Relax (feet touching)	each PB couple on their own PB couple meets PB couple	wide field of vision for B, vocal accompaniment to movement. P+B at the same head/eye level. P take up eye contact to B. contact with others (eye contact, talking, touching).
Embrace: " it's raining, it's raining, our shoulders are wet, we drip-drop with water, the wetter they get" (variation: e.g. heads, sprinkle, scoop) When B is attentive, use beaker for pouring over hands, feet, stomach and hand (approx. 3 times)	circle PB couple on their own	P observe B. attract B's attention (call name, make a noise)
Relax (sitting position): P push B to pool edge and pull them away again (variation: PP: Chalice grip) P go backwards through the water pulling B; (variation: pulling with sidewards swaying, pulling and pushing fw/bw).	row at the edge PB couples dispersed in the pool, indicate movement direction if necessary	P accompanies movement verbally (aaand, wheeee) and observes feet CI demonstrates chalice grip. Important: don't restrict shoulders; eye contact, thumb balls support chin. CI pours water over B.
Relax: offer beakers round (thimble, thimble game with feet) finishing song	open circle	CI strikes up contact with individual PB couples, says goodbye to all.

2nd lesson:
teaching the most important grips
Materials:
bowls, doll, rubber ducks

Comment:
At the beginning of the lesson the instructor should briefly run over the contents of the previous lesson. He should also explain the procedures for showering and entering the water again. Furthermore, he should enquire about the children's behaviour following the first lesson (e.g. sleeping pattern).

Abbreviations:
PP = prone position
P = parents
B = baby
CI = course instructor
SP = supine position
ri = right, le = left
fw = forwards,
bw = backwards

Phase/Duration	Objective
1 5 min	getting used to room stimulating circulation
5 min	contact to other participants, saying names
2 5 min	getting used to water loosening up of legs and arms pouring test
3 5 min	stimulate B to move by itself pouring test
4 10 min	singing introduction of materials free playing finishing up

Contents/Method	Organisation	Teaching method
wandering through the pool in heart-to-heart grip: "We're wandering, we're wandering and will meet again at the 'red' pool edge" (variations: yellow, green, at the steps etc. We're flying, we're jumping towards the edge, confrontation)	Mark pool edges with different-coloured swimming boards.	B has wide field of vision, P point its attention to water/pool edge. P + B are at same head/eye level, P-B eye contact.
"Hello Ellen, hello Ellen we're swinging to you, hello Ellen, hello Ellen first us and then you". Trophy (vertical)	One PB couple in the circle, outer circle moves in toward them/ away from them.	striking up contact with others (eye contact, talking and touching), introduction of parents after each other.
Embrace: wat-er-waves (3 times) pull their outstretched arm in front of them through the water and push the waves towards B's chest, ri/le shoulder and pour drops of water over its head.	Circle	P and CI talk to the movement, observe B.
Relax: "like a ship on the sea rocking here, rocking there" (SP: let legs be moved by water current, variation: arms).	Circle	P turn their upper body to le/ri.
Embrace: with the bowl pour water over B's hands, feet, stomach and head (approx. 3 times)	PB couple on their own, CI goes from couple to couple	P and CI observe B's behaviour.
Chalice/basket: P go backwards pulling B. CI splashes water onto B's back or churns water underneath its body. CI assesses B's attentiveness and pours water over B's head (approx. 3 times)	dispersed in pool, going in one direction. going past CI (tunnel)	CI demonstrates and corrects grips. P stimulate B to movement. CI demonstrates and explains pouring test (doll).
Embrace: 'ducks in the water'. P guide the duck past B – to and fro, back and forward (tickling game), up and down, offer it. Variations/Other ideas: "duck driving" "duck hunting", "duck dance" around the duck	dispersed in pool	CI suggests game and then takes up contact with each PB couple.
finishing song	circle	CI says goodbye to all.

101

3rd lesson:
pouring technique in more detail, demonstration of diving technique

Materials:
bowls, rubber rings, swimming mats

Comments:
Participants can begin the lesson themselves (getting used to room). The lesson begins in a circle with a short discussion and the teaching of a group activity.

Abbreviations:
PP = prone position
P = parents
B = baby
CI = course instructor
SP = supine position
ri = right, le = left
fw = forwards,
bw = backwards

Phase/ Duration	Objective
1 5 min	stimulate circulation
5 min	take up contact with neighbours (to the right and left)
2 5 min	getting used to water
	loosening up of legs and arms
3 5 min	B's movement by himself
	pouring test and diving
4 10 min	introduction of materials
	development of free play
	finishing up

Content/Method	Organisation	Teaching method
Embrace/Confrontation in alternation: "Look around, hello (3 times), now let us all begin. Begin to swing (3 times)...." Variation: dance, turn Trophy (vertical): "Hello neighbour, hello neighbour we're coming towards you, hello neighbour, hello neighbour first far away and then right beside you."	Circle Two PB couples (ri/le neighbour) turn/move towards each other (repeat again with other neighbour)	B has wide line of vision, P+B are at the same head /eye level. P take up eye contact to other B. Contact taken up with others (eye contact, talking, touching). Saying one's names.
Embrace: "It's drizzling, it's raining, a storm is brewing". P play on water with fingers, sprinkle water over B's head and churn up the water with the whole arm. Relax: wriggle and jiggle rhymes. Variation: Leg tunnel: leading the arms	Circle, CI in the middle of the circle Circle	P and CI talk to the movements, turn upper body. P guide B's legs/arms; give it time to move by itself
Chalice/basket: P walk bw pulling B and push the child feet first towards the wall ('parking') Variation: Waiter's tray. CI splashes water onto B's back or churns up water underneath it. CI assesses B's attentiveness and then pours water over its head (approx. 2 times), depending on reaction to pouring test, brief diving under.	dispersed in the pool walk around with a tunnel route alongside the pool edge	CI demonstrates and corrects grips. P encourage B to move. CI demonstrates and explains pouring test and diving with the aid of a doll. CI and P observe B's behaviour.
Mat meeting: P hold B in embrace grip, slap or push water onto the mat. Relax: lay B's legs onto mat, pull away again, let it kick against it. B's hands on mat, touch and go away again. Armring:P's hands holding the edge of the mat, rings on the mat for B to play with. finishing song	dispense around the mat(s) circle	CI takes up contact with individual couples. CI says goodbye to all.

6.2.1 Forms of Basic Movement and Organisation in Water

In order to make parent-child swimming rich in variety one should be aware of the great number of possible movements available which can be adapted for water. Parents can walk, run, hop, gallop, twist, jump, and turn and vary these movements forwards, backwards and sideways as well as up and down.

These directions can be altered through specific instructions (e.g. curves, eight shapes, bow shapes) or by changes in dynamics (powerfully – lightly), speed (e.g. fast – slowly) or rhythm (e.g. short-short-long). By being moved around the child learns different rhythms of movement and its ability of orientation is trained. Songs, rhymes or music (e.g. from a tape recorder) rhythmically support movement coordination.

In order to loosen up, vary and structure the group according to its objectives, a variety of organisation forms can be chosen:

◆ In the so-called *free room* an unforced style of movement is possible when the parents are moving forwards or sideways with their eyes in the direction they're heading in. For grip techniques where the parents walk backwards it is advisable to indicate the direction so as to avoid bumping into each other.

◆ The *circle* is particularly suitable for starting and finishing off a lesson as well as for current and maelstrom activities.

◆ The *couple* formation (parent-child) enables intensive eye contact as well as games with facial expression and parts of the body.

◆ By *forming a passage* the child-to-child contact is intensified with each parent-child couple standing opposite each other.

◆ By *forming a snake* touching or horse-riding games can be tried out on the parent in front. For running games the snake can be changed to a snail so that all participants are quite near to each other.

◆ A *circuit course* can be set up – adapted for the swimming pool form – where both parents and children are able to orientate themselves. There is no fear of wrong-way drivers.

◆ *Diagonally* or with a contrarotating *double-circle* it is possible to greet all participants individually.

◆ Suitable for the edge of the pool or the steps is when the parent-child couples *line up in a row*. Depending on the exercise one should ensure there is sufficient distance between each couple, by having them stand and work on two opposite sides in sequence.

Parent-child couples can play in small groups and – after a getting-to-know phase – can venture a short child-swopping activity.

In order to give the parents with their children some orientation guides it is wise (from a methodical aspect) to make use of certain items, e.g. street marking cones, ropes, mat tunnels, washing lines, coloured boards. They make explaining easier and cannot be missed.

THE GRIP-ABC

6.2.2 The Grip ABC

Holding and carrying grips are a significant part of the lesson. By explaining and practising the grips the parents learn to feel safe and secure with their child in the water.

The child, a non-swimmer who is dependent on supervision and support in the water, should feel safe and sound with the weight-bearing capacity of parental hands, so as to experience this adventure in water without any fear or discomfort. A child will only start becoming curious in a secure atmosphere and want to discover its environment.

Different physical conditions reign in water compared to on dry ground. Buoyancy force makes postural and movement work in horizontal position easier in water. However because of its physical proportions, lack of muscle strength, uncoordinated mass movements and difficulties with orientation, the long-term holding of its head above the water involves a great amount of performance and effort for the child. In order to secure and ease its head position one should hold the child in a diagonal forward-leaning position (45°). One places one's hand under the chest where the centre of gravity is.

This position enables the child to have a free and three-dimensional scope of movement, eases its efforts to get upright and widens its radius of perception. The child quite likes this position and keep it up for a relatively long while.

Criteria for grips

Grips are there to secure the child, i.e. the child's missing forces of buoyancy and locomotion have to be supplemented with a parent's hand. The child's head must be well above the water surface (no water is swallowed), without the child having to overstretch (no horizontal lines on his back, feet are in the water).

The grip must be firm enough so that the child feels held, but loose enough to prevent its body and scope of movement and action from being restricted (particularly in the shoulder area).

The parents' holding activity should be adapted according to the water's buoyancy force and the child's own holding and movement strength. The grips are implemented corresponding to the child's motor development and should take its favourite position into consideration.

Up to his sixth month a child cannot yet lie in prone position for a long time; it feels just as comfortable in supine and lateral postion. As verticalisation sets in the child prefers an almost completely upright position so that it should be held *standing up*.

The lesson should be methodically structured according to the degree of difficulty of the various grips so as not to overtax the parents. At the beginning of the course grips using both hands are easy and secure for practice and use, the single-handed grips on the other hand are better for later on when one feels safer and more self-confident with the child.

Any grips which involve and demand more muscle strength and concentration should be alternated with simpler, easier grips so as not to get tired or tensed up oneself.

One must pay particular attention that the parents are up to their shoulder in water. It is important that parents' and children's eyes are at the same height. This conveys closeness, security and trust (exception: when the child is in supine position). The parents have to focus their eyes on the child's face in order to be able to check where it's looking to as well as observe its sensations.

Grip techniques and expressions

One differentiates between single- and double-handed grips in prone or supine position and in sitting or standing position. Lateral position is only used as a temporary position of 'handling' or as an exercise for balance stimulation.

The parents' duties are to secure the child with their hands and their eyes, regardless of their position to the child: front on, from the side or from behind.

All expressions describe the position to the child and where its body is being supported. They are given short and snappy names making them visually imaginable especially for course purposes. The description and visual presentation is deliberately in mirror image for some grips so as to let the person demonstrating decide for himself which hand to put where.

The grips are always described and illustrated from the 'confrontation' starting position. Left-handed persons must proceed in mirror image. Besides age-specific pre-requirements, the handling, advantages and disadvantages of the grip as well as ideas for play activities are described in each case.

Suitable Age

The frontal carry grip is suitable for coming into the swimming pool with babies under six months. Children of this age still need stabilisation of the head and body as well as body contact, which is guaranteed with a large proportion of the baby's body resting against the mother's body. One seldom uses this grip for the beginning of a lesson with older babies, as they insist on turning towards the water immediately and because of their weight are carried on the hip and faced towards the water.

Handling

The children are placed on the adult's chest and are able to look over his shoulder. It is advisable to carry the child slightly to one side so as to have the other hand free for holding onto the rail when going into the water. With the lower arm the baby's body is held at the parent's chest; the elbow is at the same level as the child's bottom; the widened hand supports the baby's head and shoulder areas. Babies particularly enjoy being carried on the parent's heart side as the close contact enables them to feel the heartbeat; body warmth is exchanged and the child feels safe and attached (cf. fig. 1).

Application

Due to the close skin contact the child becomes familiar with the strange situation slowly and carefully. The parents walk around the pool talking quietly to the child who gets various different opportunities to observe things and whose body is being gently washed by the water. Depending on how one can enter the pool and how deep the water is, one gradually lets the water come to shoulder height (baby's and parent's). While one arm is holding the child, the other hand can wet the baby's back and massage it lightly, naturally.

Advantages and disadvantages of the grip

Parents may find this grip to be of disadvantage as the baby's movement activity is restricted. However it proves to be worthwhile using this grip for the first few lessons as one is enabled to consciously start off a lesson with a lot of body contact, which in turn encourages both parent and child to feel secure. It should be the routine grip for the beginning of every lesson. A head-to-head position is good for stabilising very young babies' heads. The grip holds the upper body steady but not the legs. The child can observe its environment by looking over the parent's shoulder and through its behaviour shows its parents its urge for activity, i.e. when the right time has come for to move it out of this careful, close position; it straightens up, lifts its head and turns its upper body around.

Comments

One must point out to the parents that they are to carry their child at head level so its view is not blocked. As the child briefly gets worked up at chest level due to deeper breathing caused by the water pressure, and because of the effects of the temperature on it it must be dipped into the water very slowly.

Fig. 1: Heart-to-heart

Game ideas:
- To and fro: rocking from side to side, dipping in as far as the cheek, humming along.
- Up and down: moving up and down, dipping in as far as the shoulders, accompanying it with words ('1-2-3', down, '1-2-3 up).
- Movement verse, e.g. "we're going to turn round, then going to bend down, now we stand up straight again, and the dance can begin again".

Suitable age:
This grip is used from six months onwards.

Handling
The child is seated – legs straddled – on the adult's hip, so that its upper body is pointing to the front and both its hands are able to move around freely in front of the adult's chest. If the child is carried on the left hip then the left hand is either grasping the child's left thigh (handle-holding position) or is around its waist. The right hand is free (cf. fig.2).

Application
This grip is suitable for entering the pool with children who are used to water when steps are available.

Advantages and disadvantages of the grip
The children have a complete view of the water and can visually comprehend the movement into water. The adult has one hand free for holding onto the rail. A disadvantage is that the baby's legs are 'stuck' in straddled position and because the arms are out in front close body contact is not possible.

Comments
One must make sure that the baby's hands are to the front thus avoiding a retraction of the shoulders.

Game ideas:

◆ With the hand that's free, draw child's attention to the water with water-splashing games (drip-drop, splashing, foaming and churning up, pushing the waves to and fro).

◆ Using the fingers of the free hand run along the water towards the baby's stomach and tickle it (e.g. hickory-dickory dock).

◆ With the free hand take hold of the baby's hand and dance (changeover of hands and hips).

◆ Greeting hands and feet (e.g. song: "We'd like to say hello to you and it goes like this – hello (splash,splash) hello (splash, splash)".

◆ Further singing and finger activities (e.g. "raindrops falling on my head").

Fig.2: Straddle

Suitable age

Open hands and clasp the baby – who is under four months – under its arms so that the tips of the index and middle fingers reach the back of the child's neck thus preventing its head from falling back due to insufficient head control. In the case of older babies the widely opened hands are holding the baby at the sides of its body so that its trunk is stabilised at the chest and the shoulders are free to move. When the baby's trunk has grown, i.e. got longer, the child is only held above the hips around the waist.

Handling

Starting out from the frontal carrying grip the child is grasped with both hands and held out in front at the same height as oneself. The fingers lie wide apart at shoulderblade level. For younger children they reach up into the baby's neck, for older children up to where the shoulderblades begin. Thumbs are lying loosely at the lower costal arch (cf. fig.3)

Fig.3:
Face to face

Application

This grip is used in the acclimatisation phase. It's used for sweeping activities against water resistance in all directions so that water flows to different areas of the body. These exercises benefit body perception and the regulation of muscle tone. If one wishes to reduce the child's stretching tone, the child is then turned in front by 90° and pushed to the left and to the right so that the baby's back receives current. To reduce the bending tone one does the same procedure with the baby's stomach. By being lifted up and down (jumping) in front of oneself its cardiovascular system is activated and legs are loosened. One can vary the effect of these exercise by varying the depths in water, i.e. how far down one goes.

Advantages and disadvantages of grip
After a certain time the hands slide into the child's underarm area, which pushes head and shoulders upwards. If the grip is kept for too long or too firmly the arms' blood supply is hindered. For this reason the grip must be corrected in between times by repositioning the hands over the hips.

Comments
With babies who aren't yet able to hold their head stably one should secure the rear head or neck area with one's fingertips so as to prevent their head from suddenly falling back.

Game ideas
- ◆ Songs: e.g. "Come little one and dance with me" / "Ringa ringa roses"
- ◆ Movement verses: "This is high and this is low" etc.
- ◆ Pushing back and forth: "Very far away and then right up close" (with blowing, bubbling)
- ◆ Jumping: "bunny rabbit"
- ◆ Pushing like a mixing bowl in a circular direction in front of you.

Suitable age

This is very suitable for babies under six months who are not able to hold their head up for long yet. Older babies (from six months on) prefer to have a free line of vision and freedom of movement in their arms in order to grasp and to splash; a reason not to put them into this position often.

Handling

Starting out from an underarm grip the parent's hands are pushed together under the chest so that the thumb balls form a triangle. The thumbs themselves rest loosely before the shoulder-joint. The parent goes backwards and as a result of this and the buoyancy the baby finds itself in prone position. The opened hands give the baby's chest expansive support (cf. fig. 4).

Application

After the acclimatisation phase of close contact and several passive flexibility and loosening-up exercises the active movement phase sets in for the child with looser body contact from now on. With this double-handed frontal horizontal grip the child is held in secure prone position so that its legs can move freely. Its double-handed nature means that it is simple and safe from toppling over, which makes it suitable for the beginning of the course/lesson as one can move around or on the spot immediately. Because of the eye-to-eye contact the child can be directly spoken to (and motivated) with the conscious use of facial expressions (mimic perception).

Advantages and disadvantages of the grip

The advantages of this grip can be seen in its simplicity and the great security it offers parents as well as in the vis-à-vis attention for the child, whose symmetrical head and body posture is being trained. If the shoulders are held too firmly the child's arm movements are restricted. Holding them too loosely restricts these movements even more.

Comments

One must ensure and point out that the parents are up to their shoulders in water so as to be on the same eye level as their child; it's advisable to call out this instruction. Many parents are not able to stay standing with their legs bent in the water for long.

Fig. 4: Chalice

Game ideas:

◆ Parents make bubbles in the water, the children watch. The parents snort at the baby's stomach (in the next exercise on the shoulders) by briefly lifting them up vertically.

◆ The parents play 'far away, up very close' and snort on the left and right shoulders in sequence (or kissing and blowing game).

◆ The parents raise and lower their arms out to the side so that the baby experiences vertical and horizontal waves at the water surface.

◆ Parents walk backwards and pull and push the child in sequence (movement verse – 'one step forward, two steps back').

Baby Swimming

Suitable age

This grip is suitable for babies under six months as the baby's body is extensively stabilised and restless, wriggly movements are secured. It is used less often with older babies as they already want to push themselves away from the adult's lower arm or turn to the side.

Handling

Starting out from an underarm grip the baby is laid sideways keeping the underarm grip with the left hand so that the right hand can move down the left-hand side of the baby's chest and the little finger is at belly-button level. Then the right hand takes on the baby's body weight giving the left hand the chance to make the parallel movement on the right-hand side of the baby's chest. The little fingers of both hands are touching at the side. Thumb and index finger are

behind the baby's underarms at the side thus preventing it from toppling sideways or slipping downwards. The parent pushes up the balls of his hands until they break the water surface. He walks backwards all the time (cf. fig. 5).

Application

This grip can be used after the phase of acclimatisation. Close contact is dropped but eye contact remains. Because of its double-handed nature the grip is easy to deal with and safe from toppling which means that it can be implemented in the early lessons. The adult and the child are able to perceive each other attentively and communicate with each other through eye contact, facial expression and soft words. As the child's trunk is evenly supported the parents can check the symmetric posture of its head and body as well as look for even, balanced movements of the arms and legs. Any tension in the trunk muscles, a child's one-sidedness or crookedness can be therapeutically "worked on" with swinging movements as well as visual and acoustic stimuli.

Advantages and Disadvantages of the grip

Carrying the child with two hands is not too exertive on the parents' muscles which means that they can keep this position up for a relatively long while and without tension. The more confident and relaxed the parents are when carrying out this movement, the freer the child is able to move. The nearness to their parent's face means that nervous children receive intimate eye contact and words of comfort; they can also touch the parent's face or lower arms with their hands. The overstretched hand position is unfamiliar and in the case of heavy children cannot be kept up for long. For older children the extent of support is too large for them to feel encouraged enough to make balancing movements. Children who are able to romp around on their stomachs at home want to have more physical freedom in the water too, to be able to turn and devote their attention to new stimuli of perception. From this aspect they find this grip restrictive.

Fig.5: Basket

Comments

One must ensure that parents are up to their shoulders in water, on the same eye level as their child. When the parents don't find the grip to be stable enough, the thumbs can be placed to the side behind the baby's underarms.

Game ideas

◆ Finger catching: parents hunt and catch child's fingers with their mouth.
◆ Fountain: parents take water into their mouth and spurt it out like a fountain, so that the child can feel the water with its hands.
◆ Stomach splashing: parents lift the child slightly above the surface and let its 'land' again in the water with a splash.
◆ Reverse parking: Parents push the child backwards towards the edge of the pool so that it touches it with its feet and then pull them away again unexpectedly.
◆ Along the wall: Parents pull the children and sporadically touch the wall with the baby's side.

Suitable age
Suitable for children from the eighth/ninth month onwards, when they have started pulling themselves up and making their first attempts climbing.

Handling
Starting out with a frontal underarm grip the child is seated on a raised knee. Then the child is offered first one thumb and then the other to take hold of. When the child is holding both thumbs the leg is set down on the ground again and the child is pulled along quickly to the side or in a circle so as to pull its legs up to the water's surface using the water resistance and the force of buoyancy. To cool down one pulls the baby towards the chest again and either offers it the opportunity to stand and climb upon the parental horizontal upper body or alternatively one can simply let the baby quieten down in this position.

Application
It can be used for a variation in movement and for singing games (merry-go-round). The children test out their postural and supportive strength, provided that their arms are slightly bent and the parents' hands are under the water surface for the child to support itself on. In a slalom run (pulling to the left and the right) water currents touch the sides of the baby's body and its arm strength is challenged.

Advantages and disadvantages of the grip
The small amount of support given is a positive factor as the water's force of buoyancy is used optimally. Depending on their motivation and other

attentiveness factors, a child can suddenly let go forcing the adult to have to catch him by his sides immediately. Because of this factor of insecurity parents prefer to hold the child's hands firmly themselves, which hinders the child's ability to hold on by itself as well as being unnecessary.

Comments
The parents should not hold on to the children, but rather the children should hold on to their parent's thumbs. The parent's fingers should be only placed loosely on the back of the child's hands.

Game ideas
◆ Sitting and hanging in sequence: The child is sitting on its parent's thigh. After verbal instructions the 'seat' disappears briefly and then moves back in again under the child's bottom.

Fig.6: Hanging swing

◆ Swing: The child is held to the side and swung back and forth so that it assumes prone and supine positions in alteration.
◆ Merry-go-round: The child is twirled around oneself or pulled in snake movements.
◆ Mountain-climbing: The parents lean back so that the child is standing on their stomach and is able to climb over the chest onto the shoulders.
◆ Holding balance: The child is standing on the parent's thigh and tries to stand by itself without holding on to thumbs.
◆ Cradle: The parents lean onto the side of the pool, sit the child onto their thigh and then swing it up and down. The thumbs are offered for taking hold of.

Suitable age
For children from 6 months on whose bodies already prove to be good and stable.

Handling
Starting out from the frontal underarm grip the baby is turned 180° and seated onto the right thigh. Then one pushes one's arms to the front under the baby's underarms and folds one´s hands together in front of the child's chest (cf. fig. 7).

Application
Make sideward swings or merry-go-round against the water's resistance. In playing phases where materials are used the child is able to grasp well.

Advantages and disadvantages of the grip
The small degree of holding work for the parents and the child's upright position are an advantage here. Children who make strange or those with a strong desire and need of body contact to their 'trust' person often turn around towards the parent and don't like being carried in this position except when they are busy concentrating on a toy.

Another disadvantage is that the parent's arm ring is so big that the parent must react and hold the child quickly when it moves out of this underarm suspension. Because of the trust person's position to the child, eye contact is hardly possible at all, it is difficult to regulate the child's head position.

Comments
Parents are able to walk upright without much holding effort. This effort would be more difficult if the parents were down a bit in the water walking forward with outstretched arms, carrying the weight in front at the water's surface.

Game ideas

◆ Finger walking: the child is held at its underarms over the parent's lower arms, the parent's fingers walk along the water and meet other walking fingers (parents).

◆ Boat: the parent's hands move forward in waves thus gently lifting and lowering the child.

◆ Crash: Bump into other parents' hands.

◆ Swinging for two: Take hold of another parent's hands and swing the children to the left and to the right.

◆ Twirling around: Stand facing another parent-child couple (eye contact). When told to "do a quick twirl" then twirl around and come back to starting position.

Fig.7: Arm ring

Baby Swimming

Suitable age
This grip is not be used with babies under five months as their body's stability and the muscular holding strength of their back muscles is not visible yet or not developed enough.

Handling
Starting out with the frontal underarm grip the child is turned 180° to the right and laid on the lower arm at stomach level. The right hand grasps the baby's waist on the right-hand side, the left hand follows suit on the other side. As the child likes to lean forward out of this position, index and middle fingers should support the costal arches (ribs) around the stomach. The child is held at a diagonal position to the water out to the side. The adult's arms should be slightly bent and held to the right so as to be able to watch the baby's head position and facial expression in an almost side profile and, if the child feels insecure, to be able to give it words of comfort with eye and skin contact (vis-à-vis) (cf. fig. 8).

Fig. 8: Trophy

Application
This grip is suitable for various games with objects for grasping, for games at the edge of the pool, interaction activities.

Advantages and disadvantage of the grip
With an open line of vision, and turned away from its 'trust' person the child can perceive other people and objects and focus on them. A disadvantage is that the child's head position is not eye-to-eye with its trust person, one must therefore pay attention that the child doesn't swallow any water.

Baby Swimming

Comments

One must point out to those holding the children that they are to carefully observe their child's head position in nearly side profile. This new independence can often lead to insecurity. In this case one must move the child's back in close to one's chest thus making it feel safe again.

Game ideas

◆ Blowing in the wind: blow holes in the water at the baby's neck, at its right and left shoulder in sequence as well as in front of it, so that the water sprays a little.

◆ Making waves: Standing in a circle with the group push the children forward and pull them back again so that a mountain of waves appears in the centre.

◆ Dolphin jumps, e.g. verses: "Little dolphins don't jump very high, bigger dolphins a little bit higher and the giant dolphins jump up sooo high and sooo far" (or with hares).

◆ Active story – slalom ride: push the child forward, include curves and lateral position.

◆ Shoulder jumps: The parents sit their child up onto their shoulders so that the child can let himself fall forward onto the water.

Double-handed backward waist grip and a double-handed frontal underarm grip for pushing the child from one person to another - Hydroplane

Suitable age
This grip is only to be used in the second six months of life when the back muscles are strong enough, the body is stable enough and the children might even be able to stretch out their arms.

Handling
Both parents are in stride position. Starting out from the underarm grip the child is turned 180° to the right and held close to one's body by the left lower arm. The right hand comes away from the child's underarm position and grasps the child around the waist. The left hand follows suit and is positioned on the left-hand side of the baby's waist. Hands are open wide, fingertips reach the costal

arches. The parent facing dips down so that his head position is at the same level as that of the child and draws attention to himself by splashing and clapping. When the child looks over, one stretches one hands out across the water surface so that it can see them. For the changeover the child is tilted forward to a 45° position and pushed over to the other person. This person takes hold of it under the arms and pulls it towards its body and prepares to turn it around and pass it back again. (cf. diag.9).

Application
This grip and the pushing along the water surface is a gliding exercise. Younger babies mainly splash around with their hands, the older ones already support the glide with leg movements. The older the child is the longer the distance that can be practised. After the children have got used to this calm passing, they can be gently thrown across (with brief underwater dive) or glided across under water.

Advantages and disadvantages of the grip
This grip stipulates the child's movements. On the other hand it promotes their ability to pay attention and their trust in both persons.

Comments
Hands should not overlap during the changeover.

Game ideas
◆ 'Hands are gone' and 'hands are back again': the person standing opposite the child shows and hides his own hands and encourages the child to come across by clapping.

Fig.9: Hydroplane

◆ "1-2-3-coming to get you": The person standing opposite the child comes with his hands toward the child (twice), the third time he grabs the child and takes it with him.
◆ "1-2-3, here I come": the child is pushed toward the person standing opposite (twice); the third time it lands on the outstretched hands.
◆ "Hello, peek-a-boo": the person carrying the child says "Peek-a-boo" and then turns around with the child, clockwise or anti-clockwise toward the front and the child is flown over to the other person. The same game is possible with the other person turning away.
◆ Docking: the person opposite holds his hands up vertically in the water. The child docks there first with its feet or its hands (twice) before being passed over.

Suitable age
This is to be used with children who are almost a year who have already managed to develop enough supporting strength through their daily crawling ventures.

Handling
Starting out from the underarm grip the child is tilted to the side and held with the left hand while the right hand moves away from the underarm area and grasps the child by the upper arm and elbow. The baby's weight is now shifted to the right hand allowing the left hand to do the same with the baby's other arm and elbow (cf. fig. 10, 10.1).

Application
This grip activates a child's support strength. It helps prepare for the use of buoyancy aids (swimming wings, rings). The parents walk backwards; the child supports this motion with its legs (instinctively or on encouragement).

Advantages and disadvantages of the grip
In the right dosage the grip improves support strength. If the exercise is done for too long, arm activity suffers because of them being in a fixed position.

Fig. 10: Hand bowls

Fig. 10.1: Underwater view hand bowls/elbows

Comments
One must ensure that parents don't drift their arms out to the side as the child cannot support itself. Hands should be positioned under the shoulders. The parents are up to their shoulders in water and their head is at the child's viewpoint. The hand bowl grip can be varied by either holding under the baby's feet or supporting the baby's bottom with one hand. These are balancing exercises for the child or can be the starting position for jumping away to the side of the pool (fig. 10.2).

Game ideas

◆ Movement song: "Hop up a little horsey, hop up again......" (gentle up and down movements when walking backwards, pulling the child).

◆ Lifting game: all the children get bigger (children are lifted slightly above the water so that they can see over their parents' head) and then smaller again (back down again).

◆ Slalom: To the left and then to the right (shifting baby's body weight from one elbow to the other in sequence while walking backwards and pulling the child); in the process verbally emphasise left and right, combining it with pressure on the appropriate elbow.

◆ Sitting balancing act: The child is balanced in the water sitting on one's hand. Near the edge it is encouraged to jump off and hold on to the edge.

◆ Standing balancing act: The child is balanced in the water standing on one's hands. Near the pool edge it is encouraged to jump down and hold on to the edge.

Fig. 10.2:
Underwater view
Hand bowls/ bottom

K Single-handed frontal prone position grip with movement stimulus through water splashes — Waiter's tray

Suitable age

Very suitable for babies under six months as their weight and the width of their chest enables them to be carried with one hand. Through the overstretching of the wrist the child's head position is able to be supported. The symmetric posture in prone position can be observed by parents for a good while and the child itself can work on this too. With older babies (from 6 months onwards) and children who are already able to turn around on their vertical axis, this position poses difficulties for the person carrying the child as the child no longer wants to stay resting on the supporting hand and, because of its weight, the child can only be held through hard strength efforts of the wrist. The child is at this stage more interested in its surroundings and wants to have a good look at them.

Handling

Starting out with an underarm grip the child is tilted over to the side into the left hand (hollow between thumb and index finger). For babies whose heads are not quite stable yet, the index and middle fingers also support the head. Remove the right hand from the child's underarm and lay it out open wide under the child's chest in such a way that the fingertips reach its belly button. The child is tilted into prone position, the left hand moves out of the underarm position and is placed on the child's neck and near the back of its head so as to stabilise the initial postural insecurity.

Fig. 11: Waiter's tray

The thumb ball of the right hand is pressed up to the water's surface so that the child's chin can be supported if necessary. The left hand ladles water onto the baby's back. This encourages the child's movement activity as well as preventing its back from cooling (cf. fig. 11).

Application

The child's movements are activated with this grip. The child moves freely with all its extremities while being supported on a small surface. Within the first six months a child is not able to balance its body weight. A sideward topple must be compensated by the parent. Older children, because of this small surface for support are encouraged to hold their balance. The direct eye-to-eye contact promotes the symmetric structure of posture and parent-child communication.

Advantages and disadvantages of the grip

This grip allows the child a great deal of freedom in movement for all limbs. As a result impulses develop for movement compensation in a bid to keep balance. A decisive factor here is the small surface for support. The hand that's free can continue to motivate and encourage the child's motor activity by splashing with the water. Parents occasionally dislike this grip.

This is due to their insecurity during the grip as particularly young babies' movements are reflex in nature, uncoordinated and restless.

Comments

The parents are up to their shoulders in water and at eye level with their child. One must pay attention that the handling is correct in the case of insecurity; one must particularly ensure that the fingers are spread out as this increases the surface of support under the chest.

Game ideas

◆ Verse: "It's drizzling, it's raining, a storm is brewing" (sprinkling head/back).
◆ Bubble song: Blowing either into the water or at the child's shoulders or hands.
◆ Back massage: Ladling water and massaging the back in circular movements.
◆ Stop and go: Walk backwards and then suddenly stop.
◆ Handshake: Lightly shake the baby's left and right hand, grasping it loosely between thumb and index finger.

Single-handed backward grip in prone position with the lower arm between the child's legs - Leg tunnel

Suitable age

This grip can be used throughout the whole first year. In the first months of life the hand that's free can help to stabilise the head from behind.

Handling

Starting out from the frontal underarm grip the child is turned 180° to the left and laid on the left lower arm, the right hand moves away from the underarm grip and is pushed forward as far as the chestbone. The hand should be open wide, supporting the chest. The left hand always changes position and can either support the baby's playing activity or his head position in the neck area. The right (carrying) arm is held at a steep angle to the water surface; the child can freely move both arms. Should the position feel insecure then it can be stabilised by bending the arm up more thus pulling the child nearer to one's body (cf. fig.12).

Fig.12: Leg tunnel

Application

This grip is to be used preferably for parent-child activites with materials, for quick forward walking with wave techniques, for songs with finger and splashing games as well as for stimulating the child's arm and leg movements by passively moving its arms with the water. If the hand that's free is placed in the neck area, the child can be pulled sideways to the left or to the right against the water's resistance so that the currents can reach its free arms as a form of body perception.

Advantages and disadvantages of the grip

This grip is popular because of the free line of vision the child has and the easy way it's carried out. A certain restriction of the child's leg movements does occur however.

Comments

The parents are leaning forward, up to their shoulders in water and are holding the child far enough out to the side to be able to see its face.

Game ideas

◆ Back massage: Smoothing out the back from the shoulders to the fingers.
◆ Hello and goodbye: Take the right arm by the wrist and shake. "Hello" and tiptoe with the fingers across the shoulders and neck to the other arm and shake: "Goodbye".
◆ Merry-go-round: Place the hand that's free over the child's neck and twirl to the left and to the right: the child's arms and shoulder are touched by the water current.
◆ Hand splashing: Place the free hand on the child's neck and on "1-2-3" lift the child up; in a slightly forwardly tilted position let it land on the water surface with its hands, making a splash. Do this in a circle or opposite another parent-child-couple.

◆ At an angle: Place one hand on the child's neck and turn the child as far as a lateral position, so as to practise holding its head in a stable position.
◆ Body turning: Place one hand on the neck and shoulder area and turn the child around sideways so that it's lying on its back. One must make sure that the child is also helping, i.e. that when lying on its side it indicates muscular efforts to change its position in the head, shoulder and leg areas. While turning keep up eye contact with the child.
◆ Rocking horse: Tilt the baby's body back and forth on the horizontal axis, i.e. from prone position to a reclined sitting position.

Suitable age

This grip should be used for a child who has had a stable head position for a while (5/6 months). One should only use it on children who indicate a willingness to become independent, as there isn't constant eye contact with the parent.

Handling

Starting out from the frontal underarm grip the child is rocked from one side to the other until it is held in lateral position by the right hand allowing the left hand to move out of underarm grip and be centrally positioned under the child's chest (hands open wide). The child is then tilted into prone position, the right hand moves out of underarm grip and is either placed across the shoulder area for stabilisation purposes or is free to move freely, ladling water. The hand holding the child should be straight in front of one's body so that the child can be observed from semi-profile. The child is to be held at such a height that no

Fig. 13: Sandwich

lines appear on the baby's back as this is a sign of the spine being overstretched; the child's chin is above the water's surface, the parents are up to their shoulders in water and at the same head level as their child (cf. fig.13).

Application

The grip is particularly suitable for aim-oriented locomotion; the water splashes encourage the child to move by itself; its limbs are free to move. To stimulate balance the child is raised and lowered. With merry-go-round games the parents can practise changing over hands. Sweeping movements against the water resistance (back and forth) make the spinal column and legs more flexible. By varying one's depth in the water one varies the strength in current on various parts of the body. This grip is also good for games at the edge (right up close and back again), contact activities with other children (near and far) and for catching and grasping a variety of playing objects and apparatus.

Advantages and disadvantages of the grip

The child has a free line of vision and freedom of movement. For parents it's a relatively easy grip. In this sideways position there is only slight strain on the wrist. With the second hand around the child's shoulder area it is possible to stabilise the baby's position, and parents also seem to find the balance and way of holding the child more stable for splashing with water than in the frontal prone position grip. However children who make strange or those in need of body contact tend to turn out of this position towards their parents and are not happy in this grip for long. Some parents find their limited view of the child's face to be a disadvantage; this however can be avoided by carrying the child directly in front.

Comments

Parents are up to their shoulders in water and either walk sideways or forwards (lower body turned) so as to constantly watch the child.

Game ideas

◆ Meeting each other and backing away again: two-parent-child couples stand shoulder facing shoulder and sweep the children in towards each other and then back out again; in the process both children should get the opportunity to touch each other with their hands or feet.

◆ Water resistance: The child is swayed back and forth through the water, its depth in the water varies which implies different current effects.

◆ Straightening up: The child is held in supine position and encouraged to straighten up (raising of the head) and turn sideways into prone position.

◆ Slowly Approaching: The child is moved forward and backwards several metres away from the edge of the pool, but more forwards than backwards, so that it gradually reaches the edge.

◆ Merry-go-round: The child is led around one's body, the movements are varied with spoken instructions such as "stop", "go on", "change hands".

◆ Shake your boogie: the child is swayed back and forth, varying the rhythm of movement and accompanying them with spoken words.

Suitable age
A universal grip for all ages as both head and body can be stabilised

Handling
Starting out with the frontal underarm grip the child is turned 180° to the right and brought to the parent's chest with the left lower arm. The left hand should be in such a position at the underarm that the baby is able to move its arms around. The right hand should be lying flat and wide at rib level. Both the child's and the adult's heads are approximately at the same level (cf. fig.14).

Application
This grip is particularly suitable for parent-child activities with playing material, for fast forward walking with wave technique, for movement songs with finger and splashing games as well as for arm and hand stimulation through passive arm movement. The hand that's free is placed at the baby's neck and its body can be pulled to the left and right against the water's resistance; its arms in particular are struck by the currents and it more consciously perceives his own body.

Advantages and disadvantages of the grip
The grip is easy to carry out. Due to the close body contact the baby's position can be stabilised. The child has an open line of vision. Eye contact and the ability to get a look at the child's face to check its reaction are limited however.

Comments

The parents are up to their shoulders in water, walk forwards while constantly watching their child.

Game ideas

◆ Stroking: Ladle water from the side onto the shoulders, stroke and smooth out the arms as far as the fingers.

◆ Hand splashing: The child is offered the parent's hand for splashing and clapping with; alternatively one can clap below the child's hands so as to motivate it.

Fig. 14: Embrace

◆ Counter currents: The child is completely embraced. The group walks around in a circle and on hearing a certain signal turn 180° so that the water current strikes against the child's chest.

◆ Rain drops, rain shower, heavy pouring rain (splash): Increase the intensity of the splashes.

◆ Making waves: Churn up the water with the outstretched hand, turning one's upper body in the process.

Single-handed frontal prone position of the child leaning on the shoulder ——————
Shoulder balance

Suitable age
This grip cannot be used until the child has acquired head stability (approx. 4 months); otherwise it is not possible to guarantee that the child doesn't swallow any water one is unable to assess where the baby's head is in this position when one is standing up to the shoulders in water.

Handling
Starting out from the underarm grip the child is laid with his chest on the parent's left shoulder and is held to her own chest with the left hand, opened wide. The lying surface (shoulder) is extended when the left arm is raised to the side or stretched out. To stabilise the baby's position the right hand is placed on the area of the child's shoulderblades or occasionally scoops water onto the child's back. The child can lean its arms on the adult's shoulder as well as splash in the water with his hands (cf. fig. 15).

Fig. 15: Shoulder balance

Application
Is suitable for the beginning of the lesson as the grip allows a lot of body contact, is a safe and secure position for the child who can get used to its surroundings thanks to the clear view it has. The grip can be varied in such a way that the parents, having placed the child on their shoulder, take hold of both its feet so as to guide them and encourage them to move by themselves (i.e. thrashing and kicking). A foot massage can also take place in this position.

Advantages and disadvantages of the grip

The parents are optimally able to observe their child's leg movements. Eye contact or a view of the baby's face to assess its reaction is not possible. As the child's arms are some of the time 'leaning' or just 'lying' on its parent's shoulder a form of lively movement is missing.

Comments

The parents walk backwards so that the baby's legs become buoyant and it is being supported in its forward movement. The parents' shoulders are just above the water surface.

Game ideas

◆ Stroking: With both hands smooth out the body from the neck to the soles of the feet. Similarly, the inner side of the baby's body is toched with a firm hand - from the chest down to the ankle.

◆ Passive Leg Kicking: Take hold of the baby's thighs with both hands and move its legs up and down in sequence or simultaneously and with breaks, where the baby can still 'feel' these movements.
◆ Active Leg Kicking: By splashing water, by tickling or pressing on the baby's feet its legs are encouraged to start kicking.
◆ Foot Massage: Massage its feet with the thumbs.
◆ Leg loosening and gymnastics: Place hands alongside the baby's body and move its legs up and down out to the side. If an older child props its hands up on the parent's shoulder then one can also raise the legs up far enough or the child to be in a handstand position.

Single-handed sideward prone position grip with upper arm support on the parent's lower arm - Merry-go-round

Suitable age
To be used in the second six months as the shoulder girdle is then strengthened with enough muscles. The grip should only be used with children who already focus in on their surroundings and strive for independence.

Handling
Starting out with the frontal underarm grip the child is turned 90° to the right; its chest is placed on the parent's underarm so that the baby is now in prone position. The thumb and index finger of the left hand form a ring around the baby's upper arm. This ring must be loose so as not to hamper blood circulation. The right hand moves out of the underarm grip and can stroke the

baby's back with water. The hand holding the child is directly before the parent's body so that it is possible to observe the baby's posture, the direction it's looking in and its facial expression in semi-profile. While holding the child up in this way one should not see 'wrinkles' on its back as this is an indication of an overstretched spinal column. It is important that the parents are up to their shoulders in water and both heads are at the same level (cf. fig.16).

Application
This grip is suitable for massaging both the feet, neck and back areas as well as for encouraging leg activity through guided leg-flexing movements. The hand that's free can either splash with water and invite the child to move by itself or can take hold of the baby's thigh around the hip to raise the child up (flying games). By laying this hand on the back of the baby's head it can be brought into the calming supine position (Relax (S)).

Advantages and disadvantages of the grip

The grip offers the child freedom of vision and leg movement. The upper arm ring stabilises the child's position; there are hardly any balancing difficulties or insecurity in posture when the lower arm is held parallel to the water surface and pulled along. Children who make strange or those in need of body contact often turn around towards the parents and cannot be kept in this position for a long time. The adult requires static holding strength for this grip as it is carried out with an outstretched arm (long lever). The upper arm ring hampers freedom of movement in the child's arms. Constant eye contact is not possible.

Fig. 16: Merry-go-round

Comments

The parents move forwards or sideways through the water. The upper arm ring can also be undone by pushing the hand right through beneath the underarms so that it stabilises and supports the back of the lower arm.

Game ideas
◆ Dolphin wave: Place the free hand on the child's bottom; push it down gently and let it rise up again.
◆ Aeroplane: Place the arms under the baby's arm and hip-joints, raise it up and let it land on the water, thus activating its skin and legs.
◆ Leg shaking: The free hand gives the closest leg a shake (change hands).
◆ Stroking: Stroke and smooth out both the upper and lower side of the baby's body from the head down to the feet or stimulate it with a whirlpool.
.

Suitable age
To be used particularly in the first months of life (up to four or five months), as children of this age are better able to stabilise their body in supine position without requiring any strength for holding their head up. If the child is able to turn by himself from supine position into prone position, it often refuses supine position in water. This comes back again after the first year.

Handling
The child is in the frontal carrying grip on one side. The left hand extensively supports the baby's back both in the shoulder and lumbar region. The right hand

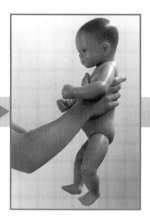

goes diagonally across the body and grasps the child's outer (right) shoulder. A ring is formed with the thumb and index finger. The lower arm supports the back of the baby's head. The child is then brought into supine position around the vertical axis. Its body should be lying as far down as possible in the water. Water does not come near the face, the chest area appearing out of the water is moistened. If the children refuse to have their head in the water then their head is raised so that the ears are free of water. The parent is standing upright with their head bent over the child – there is constant eye contact (cf. fig.17).

Application
Supine position is a relaxing in-between break for a child and for parents' arm relief. Besides, a child in its first year of life should have the opportunity of various stimuli of movement and position as it is not able to turn or move around by itself. In this way one prevents "one-sidedness" which can lead to faulty loads or orthopedic problems. In supine position the child's perceivable

visual stimuli are reduced. Buoyancy is particularly good in the supine position relieving the muscles and joints. The child perceives this physical change via its senses, a change which in turn stimulates its skin and positioning senses (balance organs, skin).

Advantages and disadvantages of the grip

By fixing the child in this position the grip is secure. The other hand (left) is free which is why this grip is also recommended for washing babies at home in the baby bath. However the child cannot move the arm that is being held.

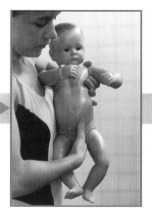
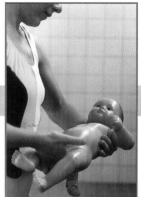

Fig. 17: Arm cradle

Comments

Shoulder ring is to be kept loose. The parents offer their child eye contact. If a child feels uncomfortable in the supine position his head should be raised (ears free of water) and the hand that's free touches the soles of the feet (skin contact) thus making the child feel safe and secure.

Game ideas
- ◆ Water cradle: Place the free hand behind the baby's (bent) knees and rock the child back and forth (towards the head and then feet).
- ◆ Near and far: Move the child into the distance away from one's own chest by outstretching one's arm (change of hands and sides).
- ◆ Kissing game: Bend over the child's face and cuddle and kiss him (touch various parts of its body with your mouth).
- ◆ Leg gymnastics. Bend and stretch the child's legs individually.
- ◆ Backgliding: Pull the child through the water (following its head), retain eye contact.

Suitable age

This grip is suitable for babies in the first few months who still like lying on their back. In the case of older and very active babies who already turn onto their stomach a lot, the situation and the form they're in that day decides whether or not they will accept this supine position. If they are playing with an object or their hands or are already a little tired, then they usually like this position which is low in stimulus. When a baby has overcome its sensitivity with water around the head then it is possible to lay the back of its head into the water.

Handling

Starting out with the confrontation position the baby is tilted to the right onto its side, and placed between the thumb and index finger; these also support the baby's neck so as to prevent its head from falling back. The left hand now moves to the back of the baby's head, the palm of the hand supports the shoulder blades and the fingers reach from the neck area up as far as the back of its head. If the child is lying calmly and balanced in the water, the right hand

can be taken away and through finger activity can be used to draw the baby's attention. The child should be deep enough in the water for only its face to be looking out. When the baby is deep in the water and lying relaxed (ears in the water) buoyancy enables it to almost hover by itself without needing much support. If the child is restless the right hand can be placed on the breastbone for stabilisation purposes. One can pull the child through the water either directly in front or out to the side, whatever one prefers.

Application

This grip is good for a rest during lesson breaks or at the end of the lesson, when the babies are tired from both the muscular efforts and stimuli. If they feel comfortable in this position with little support, then it's a sign of their trust and confidence in the water and their trust person, as well as of their ability to relax. Several stimuli are switched off in supine position and optimal use is made of buoyancy which revives the whole body.

Advantages and disadvantages of the grip

The parents don't have much muscle work holding the baby; with older and restless children this one-handed position is unsteady from time to time but can be stabilised by placing the second hand on the breastbone Children who make strange or who are in need of body contact often turn towards their parents in this position or want to feel the parent's face on theirs. There is little visual intake of stimulus in this position but in the relaxation phase this is not wanted anyway.

Comments

The parents should always be faced towards their child encouraging it to peacefully accept this position by way of eye contact, quiet words or by holding their cheek close to the baby's cheek.

Fig. 18: Water bed

Game ideas

◆ Back-haul: The child is passed from the left hand to the right, its head facing the adult's chest at all times.

◆ Backgliding: The adult walks sideways towing the child through the water by his head, constantly wetting those parts of the body reaching out of the water.

◆ Face profiles: The child is moved through the water in such a way that the parent can see it from different viewpoints, and the child has different views of the parent's face.

◆ Blowing the stomach: The child is held on one hand, the other hand is under the baby's bottom for steadiness and the parent can tickle (with the mouth) and blow on the baby's stomach.

◆ Showing feet: The child is held on one hand, the other takes hold of its leg and shows it to the child so that the child can start becoming interested in its own body.

Suitable age

As babies under six months are in the lying phase and prefer lying on their back to their stomach, it is a good idea to use the supine position often. They still have difficulties lifting their head in prone position as their muscles tire easily. Older children on the other hand prefer being in prone position as they are better able to observe their surroundings and already have the urge to practise moving around on their stomach.

Handling

Starting out with the frontal underarm grip the child is turned 90° to the right and laid on the left lower arm, allowing the right hand to change position. It now supports the back of the baby's head and the baby is now brought from prone position to supine position until its head is leaning on one's shoulder. The right hand can now be dislodged out of position and is free to move about (cf. fig.19).

Application

In this position both parents and their child are able to relax. The child doesn't have to hold its head, and the parent is spared from carrying and holding work. While younger babies enjoy lying flat in supine position older children should he held in a more sitting position as they can then see more of their environment and are then quieter. The grip can also be varied by using their 'carrying' hand to take hold of the baby's calves or the soles of its feet.

Comments

The parents' shoulders are clearly above the water so that the child does not end up swallowing water while relaxing. The child's buoyancy and the head's position on one's shoulders are more than enough to keep its body steady (without holding on) so that its head doesn't slip off the shoulders.

Game ideas

◆ Feet greeting: Standing opposite another parent-child couple the children's feet touch each other.
◆ Foot pressing: The parents hold the soles of the baby's feet so that the babies can press themselves away.
◆ Foot massage: The parents massage the soles of the baby's feet on the inner and outer edges, then its calves so as its toes are instinctively splayed.

Fig. 19: Relaxed cheek-to-cheek

◆ Toe counting:Hold up legs, touch toes individually showing them off.
◆ Leg gymnastics: The adult takes hold of the baby's calves and pushes its legs towards its stomach either in sequence or simultaneously; or he opens and closes the baby's legs above the water so that the baby can watch its legs.
◆ Rolling the spinal column: The adult takes hold of the baby's thighs and calves and swings its legs towards its head, up and down.

Suitable age

Very suitable for babies under six months because of the large supporting surface for stabilising head and body.

With babies who already prefer lying on their stomachs the position can be varied into a sitting position – with a toy.

Handling

Starting out with the underarm grip the child is laid slightly to the side, one lower arm is pushed underneath the baby's back until the inside of the hand supports the back of the baby's head like a bowl. The other arm follows suit and lies parallel under the other side of its back. The baby's feet are leaning on the adult's shoulders. One must ensure that the soles of its feet do not come into contact with the adult's chest; due to the stimulation of the soles the baby is encouraged to push itself away (cf. fig. 20).

Application

At the end of a lesson peace and relaxation are on the agenda. The baby's body needs this after all the exertion. In this grip the baby can relax physically and mentally with intensive eye-contact and kind words.

Advantages and disadvantages of the grip

Because it is held by both arms the child is in a safe, well-supported and steady position; it feels intensive skin and eye contact. On the other hand the water's power of buoyancy is not being made use of and little movement is required from the child.

Comments

The baby's bottom is at the adult's chest level. Its feet are leaning on one's shoulders or on each side of the throat. Children really enjoy the intimate words and eye contact in this position and also like using their mouth and hands to play with some toys.

Game ideas
◆ Foot nibbling: The parents grasp the little feet and guide them to their mouth.
◆ Finger sucking: The parents catch the child's fingers with their mouth and suck them.
◆ Sit down: Roll the child out of the lying position to a sitting one, with its legs to the left and right of the parent's throat.
◆ Rocking: With permanent eye contact rock the child to the left and right on the water.
◆ Whispering: Lift the child a little and whisper into each ear in alteration.

Fig. 20: Head bowl vis-à-vis

Suitable age

Suitable for children from the third month on when the baby's head is used to the water. From about the eighth month on children no longer like supine position as their growing perception encourages them to sit up.

Handling

Starting out with the confrontation position the right hand moves away and is laid flat onto the child's shoulder with fingertips lying at the shoulderblades and the thumb at the collarbone, the child's head is leaning on the lower arm.

With this grip the child is brought sideways into supine position. Similarly the left hand moves away from the baby's waist and is placed on its left shoulder, now the child is lying with its shoulders on both hands, its head is supported by the adult's lower arms and one looks down from above towards the child.

Application

In this position a baby is able to relax, its body is completely relieved of effort, its arms are free to hold an object for example and its legs can kick as much as they want. If the child is pulled through the water with snake – like movements it is challenged to make its own movements. If the child is pushed against some surface (edge of pool, hands, back, mat) or if it turns around on the horizontal axis the touching and position-changing stimuli activate toe and leg activity.

The grip should be mostly used for relaxing, to take the weight from muscles and to dim stimuli. The child's concentration is focused on its trust person who with gentle swaying, rocking songs or music is responsible for working down its physical and mental tension.

Advantages and disadvantages of the grip

The child's position in the water does not require physical work for the parents. The 'upside down' view is unfamiliar.

Comments

Holding and looking at the child from behind makes it feel close and secure. To do this the parent is approximately up to his chin in water and then touches both of the child's cheeks with his own.

Game ideas

◆ Pushing away from the wall: Push the soles of the baby's feet up to the wall until it can definitely feel it and starts pushing against it with its legs. Pull the child away with this active leg movement.

◆ Crossing a tunnel: Pull the child backwards through a holed mat for example. By playing with the fingers motivate it to look up.

◆ Meandering with tactile stimulus: Sideward meandering with changes in rhythm and touching stimuli at the side of the body, e.g. along a passage of mats or the pool wall.

◆ Cuddling: Parents walk backwards, pulling it towards one's right and left cheek in sequence.

◆ Beachball football: The parents walk forwards, pursuing a big ball which the child is meant to kick.

Single-handed carrying grip with child in sitting position for jumps with two trust persons - Armchair

Suitable age

Suitable for children from 7 months on when they have reached the stage of sitting by oneself.

Handling

Starting out with the frontal underarm grip the child is turned 180° to the left and laid on the right lower arm. The left hand moves out of the underarm grip, is flexed and is pushed in under the baby's bottom (palms up). The child is now seated on the left lower arm from the right

The child can lean back onto the parent's chest. The right hand steadies the child at its breastbone, stopping it from leaning forward. This hand is let go for the jump (cf. fig.21).

Application

This grip is recommended for use in swimming pools with unfavourable pool edges (i.e. no edge to grasp). In this position children can experience their first jumps. The supporting arm can be adjusted in height above the water's surface, i.e. there is a methodic increase in height and therefore also in the gradual structure of the exercise's degree of difficulty.

Fig. 21: Armchair

Before the jump the child is shown a visual target (e.g. other parent, a ball etc). This stimulus triggers off its motivation to move in that direction. One starts with an object that is placed on the water which the child sets his sights on. It leans forward out of its upright sitting position, is caught hold of by the right hand and brought to the object.

Instead of using an object the exercise is good with a second person who is able to observe the child and then increase the distance between them. After a good deal of practice, when the child is able to estimate this jumping distance the children can then try making a dive toward the pool edge, to the steps or to a mat which is firmly attached to something.

For this diving towards certain fixed objects it is a good idea to use soft swimming mats at the beginning. It prevents injuries in the case of wrong estimations of the distance and saves stirring up a 'fear' of injuries.

Single-handed carrying grip with child in sitting position for jumps with two trust persons - Armchair

Advantages and disadvantages of the grip

The jumping height can be greatly varied. Because children prefer jumping towards their parents rather than away from them, both parents are really needed here or a further visual stimulus at the edge of the pool.

It has come to light that when the exercise is carried out with one parent certain insecurities arise as to the choice of distance. In order to prevent injuries it is always better to go for a bigger distance; the child glides over with outstretched arms and can be given a further push from behind.

Comments

If a child is afraid it is imperative that one acts patiently; by no means is the child to be forced to tilt forwards. The parent in target should stay still so that the child can focus on him and estimate the distance before he's ready to jump.

The important thing is that the child does not just slide downwards out of the sitting position, but leans its upper body forwards, assumes the so-called belly-flop posture where the stomach lands in the water first.

Underwater view: diving under after jumping from the Armchair

Game ideas

◆ Jelly jumps: To stimulate his balance the child is moved from the armchair position and slowly dropped forward onto the front arm, and back again to the sitting position. The movements are signalled by a "1-2-3".

◆ Fish and dive: The child or the parent throws an object which can be fished back again by taking a little dive out of the parent's arm. Parents can regulate the depth the child is at and his flying span with the length of their arm. The free hand catches the child under its chest.

◆ Jumping to the mat from sitting position: On hearing "1-2-3, jump", the child jumps with outstretched arms out of the parent's arms toward the mat, where it can support himself and hold on.

◆ Jumping to the mat from standing position: On hearing "sit, stand, jump" the free hand is used for standing on and the child then jumps to the mat.

◆ Keeping balance: The child should try and balance in sitting position, i.e by seldom offering it the chance to lean back.

Double-handed frontal waist grip or sandwich grip from a sitting position ('Dropper') or standing position ('Crane') at pool edge or steps.

Suitable age
The dropper from a sitting situation is suitable for children from the eighth month on when they are able to sit by themselves. They can normally stand on their own from the tenth month on; the crane exercise can be done then.

Handling
The hands are around the baby's waist with the thumbs on the ribs and the fingers in the shoulderbade area. For the oncoming movement out of the sitting position one must make sure that the backs of the baby's knees comply with the edge of the sitting ledge; the lower legs dangle and stabilise position.

By stretching his arms out in front the child shows its willingness to move away; it's triggered off by a forward leaning of the upper body, the child's stomach nears his thighs. One must strictly adhere to this position to be completely sure that the child is away from the wall when it jumps and can't hurt himself.

Word signals prepare the child for the falling moment ("1-2-3"). It learns to anticipate it and is saved from unexpected (negative) surprises. The child shows that it expects its head to go under by closing its eyes and mouth and holding its breath. When these criteria are taken into account the child's head can briefly dive under the water by lifting it up a little later. If the child is willing to go on with this procedure the underwater period can be extended (1,2,3 seconds). If the child starts moving its legs as well it isn't picked up again until it has come to surface on its own.

When practising this exercise from a standing position at the steps one should start out having the child sitting up to its stomach in water as it can't 'jump' yet but merely leans forward or often just stays up straight. The latter can be dangerous.

If the child is still hesitant and wanting body contact the adult should offer his thumbs to hold onto. In order to avoid the child from crashing down when it falls forward the arms are outstretched and the legs are in stride position enabling an evasive manoeuvre onto the leg behind.

Fig. 22:
Dropper with
Sandwich

The parent's hands are held at the water surface for the child to support itself (not hang from) during his flight. This posture protects against injuries of the hand, elbow or shoulder joints (cf. fig. 22).

Double-handed frontal waist grip or sandwich grip from a sitting position ('Dropper') or standing position ('Crane') at pool edge or steps.

Application
The grip is for the initiation of controlled shifting and jumping.

Advantages and disadvantages of the grip
It can be dangerous when the distance between parent and child is too short; parents tend to do this out of (over-)concern for the child's safety. The child must not be pulled into the water but merely motivated and supported so that the fall occurs on its own impulse.

Doing without the supportive help is a process which is difficult to assess because of the reduced body contact. If the degree of difficulty is increased constant repetition and support is required so as to gain security and confidence.

Comments
With jumping exercises one must make sure that after the first, simple repetitions the child determines its willingness to jump itself; at the beginning the child can be encouraged and enabled to jump by clapping, splashing, holding out one's hands. Overeager children must be held back in order to get the timing right between parent and child. First and foremost safety must be guaranteed! Counting to three contributes to common safety and attentiveness.

The parents can initially stand in front of the child as he won't jump far yet and only orientates himself towards the adult directly in front of it. As the jumps get further the parents must stand in stride position to enable evasive manoeuvres. One must remember that water resistance makes a quick backward evasive movement impossible. A position to the side is better for this reason. However one must indicate where the child is to jump to (slapping water with hands) as it will only jump straight towards its parent otherwise.
    In order to promote 'long jumps' one can offer one's hand from the side.

Game ideas
◆ Dropper from sitting position, frontal: The child is sitting on the edge. One claps hands so as to draw its attention, puts one's hands around its waist and tells it to lean forward when it hears "1-2-3" in order to then fall into the water. Such a belly-flop causes water to splash onto the baby's face. If the child protects itself from this by closing its eyes and mouth, it can dip its head in briefly after a few attempts.

◆ Dropper from sitting position, sideward: The child is sitting on the edge and one hand secures its underarm, while the other hand slaps the water to attract its attention. It also perceives depth in the process. Now the parent places one hand on the child's chest and one on its shoulderblades, as in the sandwich grip, and is thus standing sideways to the child. By gently leaning back and forth and counting "1-2-3" out loud the child is encouraged to lean forward itself and fall into the water.

◆ Jumping from a standing position: When the child is already standing on its own at the edge of the pool one implements the frontal and lateral waist grip (see above). Even if the child is already able to jump in by itself one should have constant body contact with it because of the small jumping distance, particularly to protect the back of its head and back. In addition to this, the parent's hand must always be lying or slapping on the water surface to serve as a target and aid the child's orientation. Because of the danger of injury to the hand, elbow and shoulder joints one should refrain as much as possible from holding the child's hands. It's better to support its trunk.

Baby Swimming

Suitable age

The rider grip is suitable for children at the end of their first year of life who are already able to sit up on their own, whose shoulder girdle muscles are developed enough for the brief hanging by both hands and who are willing and able to hold onto their parents' shoulders when told.

Handling

The adult sits the child with its back leaning against its chest on a raised thigh. The adult's hands move away from the child's waist and offer it the index figers to hold onto. The thumb only lightly supports the back of the child's hands. By lowering his thigh the adult is holding the child in suspension and leads the child's turning movement to the left (like a turn in ballroom dancing) so that the child ends up sitting in 'piggy-back' position on his parent's back or shoulders.

After this one hand and then the other lets go of the child's hands so as to hold the child's thighs around the hip area (cf. fig. 23). As an alternative when the child is sitting in a wide straddle position the parent's hands can secure the rider position at the lower back.

The child must practise getting back down by being brought sideways near the edge of the pool; the parent knocks on the edge for gripping and by telling it what to do encourages the child to take its hands away from around the shoulders and to hold on to the edge of the pool.

Application

This grip is suitable for forms of play and movement in the warm-up phase of a lesson. By being carried in this secure position, close to the parent's body, a child has a clear view and can gradually get familiar with the water, the group and the pool itself and is moved around by the adult in a simple way.

Advantage and disadvantages of the grip

Carrying the child on one's back is very pleasant for parents as one hardly feels the child's weight here. Parents might feel somewhat insecure as they are not able to see the child's reaction and are often worried that the child might topple down from their back from leaning back or not holding on tightly enough. The child really enjoys the clear view and the close physical contact. However it often doesn't want to stay in this prone position for long as it would like to sit up and turn round and have more freedom of movement in its arms and legs.

Fig. 23: Rider

Comments

With this grip it's important that the parents are only lightly holding onto the child's hands while placing it on the shoulders. Only the child should be essentially holding on. When changing hand positions one should consciously remove only one hand first and by patting oneself on the shoulder encourage the child to hold on at the shoulders. Then and only then should the other hand let go. When practising this grip for the first time the parent must lean his upper body well forward so that the child is lying and not sitting on the parent's back initially in order to prevent the child falling backwards.

If both the child and the adult cope well with this grip, the adult can straighten up and also challenge the child to hold on with its hands and legs as well as to make compensating movements through sudden forward, backward and sideward movements. With a lot of practice a child can even secure its position on its own without any help; the parent's hands are then free to move, splash or support his own walking movements.

Game ideas

◆ Rodeo riding: With an experienced child on his back the parent leans his upper body to different sides thus provoking the child's compensatory movements.

◆ Tunnel ride: Parent and child enter low and high, narrow and wide tunnel constructions which are at various positions in the pool.

◆ Taxi: The child practises climbing on and off at various sections of the edge of the pool and on hearing the words "Climb off" and "Climb on" the child transfers over to the grips at the edge of the pool or onto the parent's back again.

◆ Car race: The parents run through the pool at various speeds or stop in between.

◆ Grand National: The parents gallop around the pool, jumping over fictitious obstacles.

◆ Waving and splashing: The parents wave or splash with their left and right hand in sequence and try to motivate the child to do the same.

Water-pouring Method and Diving

Baby Swimming

6.2.3 Water-pouring Method and Diving

The water-pouring method

One of the main objectives of baby swimming (see chapter 4.2) is *familiarisation with the water*, i.e. the child should find the time spent in the water to be relaxed, pleasant as well as being an educational and practical examination of its environment. A person's relationship with water begins in the womb.

Having gained some experience with water by practising at home (see chapter 5.2) the baby is prepared for its first day of swimming. This process is then continued here with the water-pouring method and the baby is made familiar with water's properties and effects.

Water has an effect on one's breathing and each baby has its own individual experience here and evaluates it differently from an emotional aspect. The water-pouring method assumes both a protective breathing reflex in a young baby (up to approx. eight months) and a mouth-nose reflex in a person prevailing for his entire life. These reflexes are triggered off when the face is touched with water. In order for the baby to get used to its reactive behaviour to this stimulus one carries out a gradual, step by step water familiarisation process with the help of occasional water showers over its head, paying constant attention to its emotional and physical reactions.

The water-pouring method sensitises the child in its perception of water, the aim being for it to show emotional readiness and conscious protective behaviour. On the other hand it should be desensitised to the effect that it learns to experience brief divings of its face and head under water as pleasant and stress-free situations. The parents can also be certain that their child is able to protect itself briefly. While diving techniques up to now (tapering, blowing, lifting or word accompaniment techniques) are aimed at training the baby's suitable behaviour (conditioning)

and making use of this early breathing protective reflex so that the child won't swallow or breathe in any water, the water-pouring method on the other hand assumes the theoretical concept of active learning of circumstances (perceptive learning). This means that a child shouldn't be dipped under water until it's reached an age where he knows and accepts water, i.e. takes it in visually and with touch and evaluates it according to emotion and motivation (neutral or positive): seeing, feeling, sensing, perceiving, and then processing it to be 'pleasant'.

Fig. 24: Negative reaction after water-pouring test

The water-pouring test is carried out in the first half of the lesson, when the child has got used to its water surroundings, and is on the other hand not completely tired out from the new stimuli, i.e. at a point when it is attentive and able to take things in.

When the child is used to the water a brief underwater dive triggers off a physiological reaction without any fear. For babies in the first year of life diving situations and reactions can come into being from prone position following the water-pouring test or towards the end of the first year can develop out of play situations such as flying, falling and jumping. The older the children are the more able they are to comprehend and learn to dive on their own at the steps or the edge of the pool through encouragement in the form of apparatus (material), spoken language (verbal) or by doing it oneself in front of the child (imitative).

The aim here is to give the child experience with water which enables it to adapt and protect itself without getting stressed or - as part of the desensitisation process - to lose any fears that it may already have.

Fig. 25: Positive or neutral reaction after the water-pouring test

Process of the water-pouring method for the assessment of a baby's willingness to dive:

The baby is held on both hands, in frontal prone position facing its mother or father. The instructor is standing beside the parent, says something to the baby and checks to see how attentive it is first. Using a bowl filled with water the instructor slaps the water and then pours the water out in front of the baby's eyes (at head level) within reaching distance.

Ideally the baby focuses in on this shower and puts its hand to reach it. In the phase that follows, the shower of water, keenly observed by the child (who may have to be challenged again!), is guided over its arms and shoulders towards the back of its head. At the same time the course instructor starts counting ("one") thus giving the parents a signal to watch carefully: the baby perceives the touch of water, and has a pensive look on its face at best (introverted). At "two" the water is poured over the top of the baby's head and at "three" over his face.

Ideally the baby closes its eyelids and mouth after this for a split second, then opens its eyes wide again and holds its breath for two to four seconds as the veil of water runs down its face. When the water has stopped running the baby turns its attention towards its parent or the bowl, reaches out for it and opens its mouth again with chewing movements (cf. fig.25).

The observation criteria for the baby's behaviour after this test refer to its facial expression, body language, the sounds it makes and its orientation. Negative behaviour expresses itself through a lack of orientation, an increase in muscle tension, disapproving sounds and a cold facial expression.

A positive reaction is when the baby immediately orientates itself, wants to play, shows no sign of tension and reacts happily after praise and other spoken words. A neutral result is when a child's facial expression is neither frightened or contented, when no significant muscle tension is evident and orientation returns shortly.

One can assume that a baby is willing to dive when it experiences the water stimulus consciously and without fear. This can only occur when it perceives the stimulus in a cognitive, visual and tactile way and then gives a neutral or positive 'answer' emotionally, through its facial expression and physical behaviour.

If a baby reacts positively or neutrally to the water-pouring test, then a diving attempt takes place directly after the next test (cf. fig. 26).

The willingness to dive is assessed again in every lesson and with each child as it depends on a variety of factors, although mainly on their emotional state.

The most important influential factors include the form the baby's in that day, its current stage of development, how excited it is, how willing it is to take new things in, its familiarity with the water and its level of trust, the handling and the parents' adaptive abilities as well as the course instructor's talents in observing and ability to look after the participants.

Fig. 27 Diving with the water-pouring method

One advantage of this method is the opportunity available to diagnose (assess willingness to dive), another the possibility of intervention (desensitisation of a fear of water). One can vary the test in application (much/little water).

The test is carried out without forcing the child to dive. The criteria for the assessment of a baby's willingness to dive refer to its general state and perceptive abilities, a check that its mouth closes and how long it holds his breath for.

This method ensures a baby's individual abilities and reactions at the water surface. It looks into the baby's *willingness to dive* – as opposed to the diving techniques to date which completely rely on the existence of a certain reflex and where diving takes place as a trial and error process. Negative factors are therefore not taken into consideration.

Comment: There is a whole international series of diving techniques. In connection with the water-pouring method and other techniques mentioned, the questions arise as to whether, how and in which development phases a person protects himself from water in a reflex, instinctive or conscious manner. This question has not been scientifically looked into yet. One assumes that with healthy young babies (younger than six months) the breathing protection reflex prevents water from entering the lung. Through repeated signals (blowing, splashing, lifting, verbal orders) this reflex is triggered off and trained. The baby is dipped under water for a few seconds directly after every signal. Diving occurs with the baby in horizontal or upright position (cf. BRESGES/DIEM 1981; AHR 1993; RAABE-OETKER 1998).

With older babies one talks of a conscious reaction to a signal followed by a dive under (cf. van DYK 1996). With the help of kinesthetic stimulus (lifting the child up) the baby is prepared for the oncoming dive (cf. KOCHEN/McCABE 1986).

BAUERMEISTER (1984, 65) describes how diving is consciously learned with toddlers from 18 months on. They learn it through playful instructions and imitation. HUNT-NEWMAN (1967, 42) points out how a baby instinctively holds its breath when its face is moistened with water.

CAMUS/MOULIN/NAVARRO (1994, 237ff.) assume that all persons, regardless of age, are protected from water entering their lungs by the mouth/nose reflex and the anatomy of the nose and throat area (epiglottis).

The following diagram summarises the course of procedure in the water-pouring and diving method:

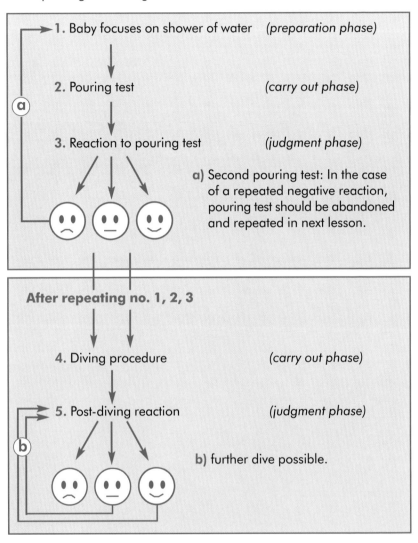

Fig 27: Course of procedure for determining willingness to dive using water-pouring method and the dive itself.

The water-pouring method is a result of observations over many years and of a separate study by the author; with its help it is possible to appropriately determine babies' willingness to dive. The method orientates itself to the baby's behaviour in each case.

Basic points on the subject of diving and diving criteria

◆ Diving can, but doesn't have to be a part of baby swimming. There are other objectives apart from getting used to the water.

◆ A certain fear of water is a natural form of human self-protection. The aim of familiarisation with water along with a short dive under is to conquer (excessive) fear of water. Short-term defence, fear or insecurity reactions are a natural part of development. Diving is then forbidden.

◆ Not all children immediately accept water splashing in their face, the foggy view, water in their ears, nose or mouth and having to catch their breath. By getting them used to these situations gently and step by step, every person can generally become familiar with or get accustomed to water.

◆ The first diving process depends less on the child's age as on its individual reaction. This reaction can be interpreted with the water-pouring test.

◆ Diving under is not compulsory, but rather a decision made by the parents - with the course instructor's advice.

◆ Before a diving prodedure the course instructor should inform the parents on its advantages and disadvantages. The diving techniques themselves should be explained in such a way that the parents become familiar with this situation, i.e. develop confidence in their own abilities as well as in the abilities of their child.

◆ The first diving attempts are to be carried out by the parents under the course instructor's guidance and are not tied to a specific depth or duration.

◆ There is no reason to insist with all force on carrying out diving exercises regularly for fear that the child will forget what to do. Diving should be positively experienced and learned and the child's reaction and acceptance of it must be tested again in every lesson. Diving is taboo when a child is in bad form or going through an emotionally difficult phase.

6.2.4 Movement Exercises

One differentiates between passive movement exercises where the child is being moved through the water by its trust person, and active movements where the child through playful stimulus and motivation is challenged to move by itself.

Passive movement exercises

These movement exercises, taken from the exercise catalogue (by CHEREK 1984) and extended by a few ideas, consciously use water resistance and buoyancy as a stimulus or aid to movement:

◆ Rhythmic raising and lowering of the child in the vertical position (hopping) – to loosen up the legs.

◆ Sidewards swinging with the child in prone or supine position (slalom) for stretching the sides of the body.

◆ Raising and lowering of the child in a horizontal position with and without active pressure on the shoulder (wave movement) – for straightening up the spinal column and making it flexible.

◆ Shaking the child's legs while in supine position with its head leaning on one's shoulders – for loosening up the legs.

◆ Sidewards swaying in the vertical position, either frontally or with the child turned 90° so that the back (flex tone) as well as the chest (stretch tone) are struck by the current – for regulating muscle tone.

◆ Pushing and pulling of the child in underarm grip (prone/supine position in alternation) – practice of holding up the head.

◆ Circular touching of the child in vertical position – for making shoulder and hip joints more flexible.

◆ Turning of the child in vertical position around the vertical axis in hip grip (twist) – for loosening shoulder girdle.

◆ Child in supine position with its head leaning on one's shoulders; then the raising and lowering of legs (roll-up) – for making the spinal column more flexible.

◆ Child in supine position with its head leaning on one's shoulders: adult's hands are on the child's bottom or hips so as to gently raise and lower its body as well as rock it sideways – for regulation of muscle tone. The same can be done in prone position (shoulder balance) with the child's lower arms holding on to its parent's shoulders.

6.2.5 Games, Playing Apparatus and Material

Spending time in water is almost a substitute for other forms of playing apparatus as the water itself, the swimming pool and the group represent a number of opportunities for play. The more grasping abilities a child develops the more interested it is in discovering its surroundings.

Some play ideas without the use of apparatus or material are described as follows.

Circle and group games
◆ Swopping places: (all babies under six months change places). All change for heaven: - by crossing through the circle. "There's room on my right,on my right". Parents wink to each other.
◆ Passing on games: (child is passed around with song). Parents pass a ball or a doll around the circle, the children watch movement.

Interaction games between parents and child
◆ Touching games (tickling, stroking, bubbling, blowing).
◆ Singing and finger activities.
◆ Flying games.
◆ Gymnastics games.
◆ Hopping and horse-riding games (on one's thighs: "hop up a little horsey...").
◆ Rocking-cradle activities.

Interaction games with other children
The aim here is social learning and the development of group behaviour; the children perceive and play with each other.
◆ "Flutter, flutter, on we go, we're flying high, then flying low, first it's me then it's you, this is what we like to do".
(Two children opposite each other.)
◆ "I hop and hop and hop on only one leg, and when I'm tired and can't go on then it's time for Sally to join along, I hop and hop and hop on only one leg".
(Two children opposite each other in alteration.)

Games for the senses: seeing - hearing - feeling

These games promote 'sensitisation' of the senses and improve the sensory motor identification performance (sensorimotor integration). Working with contrasts is a good idea for developing sensitive perception. With the use of opposites one can discover themes when preparing a lesson and select items for creating play and adventure activities:

◆ bright and dark (e.g. tunnel rides)
◆ soft and hard (e.g. sponges and pot scrubbers)
◆ round and square (e.g. balls and dice)
◆ light and heavy (e.g. full and empty bottles)
◆ float and sink (e.g. balloons and water balloons)
◆ transparent and opaque (e.g. different marbles or balls)
◆ rough and smooth (e.g. tiles and then gaps in between)
◆ uneven and prickly (e.g. differently structured balls)
◆ big and small (e.g. small rubber rings and big hoops)
◆ shiny and dull (e.g. gymnastic wands and pool ladders)
◆ curvy and straight (e.g. ropes and wands/sticks)
◆ long and short (e.g. pool tubes and connecting pieces)
◆ high and low (e.g. high and low washing lines)
◆ loud and quiet (e.g. empty shampoo bottles and gravel-filled ones)
◆ dry and wet (e.g. cloths)
◆ warm and cold (e.g. several buckets filled with water at different temperature).

Typical game forms

◆ "Loud-loud-loud psssst" (quiet): splashing and kicking in the group circle and then stoppong and listening.
◆ "Hello, hello, peeeep": hiding behind a washing-line which has cloths hanging on it.
◆ Musical statues: playing music (e.g. from cassette recorder) and then stopping it- everyone has to then stand still.
◆ Rhyme: "water-beetles, water-beetles running here and there, water-beetles, water-beetles, it's the tummy (head, neck etc) they prefer".
◆ Walking alongside the wall (feeling tiles and cracks etc).

Playing apparatus and materials

Playing apparatus and materials stimulate a baby to move with or on top of the objects, to test them out or discover them. In a lesson they help in the familiarisation process and can occasionally be used to support buoyancy.

Playing material must be safe in texture, suitable for water, hygienic and storable. In compliance with the methodic structure of the lesson they are offered for use (in the right dosage) after the children have got used to the water and after exercises (loosening up, diving). They should be compatible with the children's current stage of development (physical, motor, mental) as well as that of the sense organs, i.e. they should not overstimulate.

When selecting large and small pieces of apparatus one must remember that large apparatus often overtax a baby and that it will not accept all items. In practice it has proved worthwhile to introduce a baby to new apparatus and playing materials step by step and not just confront it with it (e.g. swimming mat).

The following pieces of apparatus and playing materials are suitable for motivating and creative activities:

◆ avtivity mats (with numbers and letters)
◆ airbeds
◆ artificial grass pieces

◆ balls (massage, soft, tennis, beach, slow motion, colourful plastic balls for blowing around)
◆ balloons
◆ building blocks

◆ beakers
◆ bedsheets
◆ boats (blow-up)
◆ brushes
◆ bells
◆ baths (baby baths) and buckets
◆ bicycle tubes
◆ blowpipes

bottles (shampoo, squirt or spray)
◆ bowls
◆ clothes line and clothes pegs
◆ cork chains
◆ coffee filters

◆ ducks (or other plastic animals)
◆ duplo bricks

◆ face cloths
◆ frisbees
◆ funnels

◆ garden tubs (water-butt with the base cut out to make a tunnel)
◆ globe forms (either on the swimming rope or filled transparent balls)

◆ hair curlers
◆ holed raft (swimming mats)
◆ hoses/tubes (transparent, with different widths, thin for breathing exercises, thick for sticking into water inlets to make a fountain)

◆ ice cubes
◆ islands (garden chairs or tables with weights)

◆ 'Kinder surprises' (attached together, e.g. as a chain)

◆ laundry tubs
◆ lego bases (for feeling)
◆ lids

- mats (with holes, swimming mats, insulating mats, gymnastic mats)
- mirror (plastic board with mirror foil stuck on)

- painting brushes
- paddling pools (blow-up)
- plastic packaging with air cushions
- pool tubes (with connecting pieces)
- pot scrubbers
- pull buoy

- rattles (shampoo bottles filled with gravel)
- rings (tennis, diving)
- ropes
- rubber gloves (for medical use)
- rubber rings (gymnastic, swimming)
- rubber suction instruments (for dividing space up)

- skittles
- slide (plastic or a swimming mat with plastic covering)
- soup ladles
- spinning tops
- sponges (cosmetic or body)
- spoons (cooking spoons or tea-spoons)
- sprinkler (for clothes)
- sticks (gymnastic, diving, broomsticks)
- stiroform rings (covered wih nylon stockings)

- squeaky toys
- swimming board
- swimming wings
- swimming bars (alternative: sticks/poles with swimming wings stuck onto the sides

- tea towels
- tennis ball tins
- tubs (yoghurt, margarine, camera film)
- tubes
- tulle
- tunnel (out of material or water-butt without base)

- UFOs (egg flips)

- vitamin cylinders (filled with gravel, sand)

6.2.6 Rituals, Poems and Songs

(passed on, altered, thought up during lessons, learned in seminars,.....)

The following examples are translated from the German. A melodic and ryhthmic translation is of course only possible up to a certain extent. These poems and songs are therefore meant to give you examples and inspirations for your own lessons.

Greetings and getting to know each other
◆ "Look up, look up we're as high as a tower – and now it's time to start the hour."
◈ "Hello, hello how nice it is, how nice it is that you're here today. x-x is here, x-x is here, and x-x is here, now we're all here, let's give a big cheer!"
◆ "We want to say hello and we do it like this: hello (splash, splash), hello (splash, splash)."
◆ "We're sailing on the Thames (x-x) where the ships go round and round, the ship's name is (parent) and (child's name) is homeward bound."
◆ "Come over here, hello, hello, come here and give a smile,
come over here and clap your hands stay with us for a while.
Come over here the music's on come here and sing this song,
come over here, jump in the air, now come and jump along!
Come over here, we're over here all babies big and small,
come over here, kick all around , c'mon we're having a ball!"
◆ "Look around and say hello, now we can begin. We begin to dance and dance, we're da-an-cing (swing, twirl,...)."
◆ "Hello Ellen (x-x), hello Ellen we're waving to you, hello Ellen, hello Ellen, we're all here with you. "(A parent-child couple in the middle, turning around slowly).
◆ "Good morning, good morning I'm waving to you, good morning, good morning, and you're waving too." (Alternative: nodding, splashing, kicking.)
◆ "Hel-lo, hel-lo, come straight over here, let us start singing, dancing and swimming, hel-lo, hel-lo come straight over here."
◆ "Hip hip hooray, it's swimming time today, I'll go right over to my friend so we can swim round every bend, hip hip hooray it's swimming time today."

◆ "We're going on a cruise and we're waiting to depart, whoever wants to sail with us had better make a start. You and you the two of you, don't need to stay at home, I'll get the others in a jif and then we'll sail to Rome."

◆ "Puff, puff, puff goes the big steam train and now it's Ellen (x-x) driving, she's taking us as far as Cologne (x) and now she goes behind."

◆ "Puff, puff, puff, goes the big steam train a tunnel's round the bend, I don't like driving on my own so I take all my friends."

Getting used to the water and stimulating circulation

◆ "It's raining, it's raining it's raining night and day, and if it doesn't stop so soon, we'll all be rained away."

◆ "Splish and splash, the rain comes down, on my hair and on my nose from my nose down to my toes, it stops a bit and makes no sound, and then it splashes on the ground." (Slap water with hand.)

◆ "When my fingers are wide awake, what wriggling and jiggling they do, they're playing on the water now, doo-bee-doo-bee-doo."

◆ "Oh the grand old Duke of York........."

◆ "Hop up a little horsey, hop up again......"

◆ "The big ship sails on the alley, alley o...."

◆ "Frogs in the night are so lonely, frogs in the night they want only, to swim in the pond, along comes Mr. Bond, and then it's ribbity ribbit, hoppity hop, ribbity ribbit, shwoppity shwop."

◆ "I'd like to swim, come swim with me, it's no fun on my own you see, better is when you swim with me, swim, swim swim you and me." (Variation: splash, sprinkle.)

◆ "We're splashing water all around, not so loud, without a sound, this is how we like to splash, splash all around." (Variation: kick, jump.)

Stimulating senses of lying and position

◆ "All the ships in a row rocking to rocking fro."

◆ "Big grandfather clocks go tick-tock, tick-tock; small clocks go tic-ka, toc-ka, tic-ka, toc-ka, tiny little clocks go tickatocka, tickatocka, tickatocka and the alarm-clock goes bbbbbbrrrrr."

◆ "I fished, I fished the whole night through, I didn't catch one fish, just you."

◆ "Rocking the angels, rocking the angels up into the sky (lift and throw)."

◆ "High and low, fast and slow, heavy and light, dark and bright."
◆ "Back and forward, right and left, up and down, right and left."
◆ "Turn around, turn around, first this way then the other way." (Turn the child's direction by throwing him up (left/right) with both hands and changing hand position.)
◆ "I'm a jumping jack, so I am, and I can move both arms and legs, so I can, first I jump to the right, to the right, then jump to the left, to the left, then I fly so high, so high and then I sink right down, right down and turn myself around."
◆ "I have a big red balloon, and I'm going to lose it soon, it flies higher and higher over the town, I pull its long string then it comes back down."
◆ "Ten green frogs hopping near the wall............"

Feeling one's body
◆ "A little snail, a little snail creeps up, creeps up, crawls back down, crawls back down, tickles my tummy, tickles my tummy."
◆ "Hickory, dickory dock....."
◆ "Hokey cokey" (with children, parts of the body).

Activating leg movements
◆ "Good morning legs, what are your names? My name' s Jiggle, my name's Wriggle."
◆ "Show your feet and show your shoes then watch the water babies move: They're kicking, (hop, turn) they're kicking, they're kicking all day long (twice)." (The group moves in and out together in the circle; the children's feet touch each other in the centre.)
◆ "When my feet are wide awake what wriggling they do, they wriggle in the water, doo-bee-doo-bee-doo."
◆ "How high can a flea jump? He can jump this high!" (Child's feet touch adult's thighs/stomach.)
◆ "The children are happy, having great fun, kicking in water, one after one."

Soothing - rocking-cradle song

◆ "All the ships in a row rocking to rocking fro."

◆ "Rock-a-bye-baby......"

◆ "Hush little baby, don't say a word, mama's gonna buy you a rocking bird...."

Saying goodbye

◆ "Now we're all wet through we played in the water me and you, we'd so much fun swimming around and now it's over, we're homeward bound, until next week stay fit and well, there's more fun then, that I can tell."

◆ "This is the way we say goodbye, say goodbye, say goodbye, this is the way we say goodbye when we're finished swimming."

◆ "When the moon is in the sky and when the sun has said goodbye, we are finished for today here's a kiss for on your way."

6.3 Swimming Aids

Swimming aids can basically be used from the tenth month onwards when the child already possesses its first balance reactions and has developed supportive capacity in its shoulder girdle through its practice in crawling. If swimming aids are to be used at all, then always for a very brief time so as to stick to the main objective of baby swimming – a common activity of movement for parent and child – and restrict a baby's freedom of movement as little as possible.

From a methodic aspect the following points must be considered when using swimming aids:

◆ Body contact and the associated natural trust basis and dependence between parent and child is no longer present; this occurs at a time when a baby indicates a strong need for close contact and likes to be held and carried.
◆ This buoyancy apparatus changes the baby's natural position.
◆ A swimming aid leads a baby to believe that it can swim alone.
◆ Parents tend to ease off with their constant supervision.
◆ The child's freedom of movement is restricted.
◆ They encourage a child's passive movement behaviour.
◆ When used regularly a child gets into the habit of only trusting the swimming aid in the water.

A course instructor should discuss the use of swimming aids with the parents in the lesson or introduction so as to make them aware of the advantages and disadvantages of buoyancy aids and give them practical advice on their purchase and use. Advantages of swimming aids are:

◆ A child is able to move by itself.
◆ It practises holding its balance.
◆ It exercises its supporting ability.
◆ It actively moves towards chosen targets.
◆ It can change its position and direction by itself.

The most widely used swimming or buoyancy aids for babies are swimming wings (arm bands), rings, sticks or pool tubes with connecting pieces (see addresses in appendix). Jackets, belts, cushions aren't used until a later age.

IV APPENDIX

7 References

AHR, B. (1993): Schwimmen mit Babys und Kleinkindern. (Spielerische Übungen zur frühzeitigen Bewegungsförderung im Wasser). Thieme: Stuttgart.

AHRENDT, L. (1997): The Influence of Infant Swimming on the Frequency of Disease during the First Year of Life. In: ERIKSSON, B.O./ GULLSTRAND, L.: Proceedings of the XII FINA World Congress on Sports Medicine. Chalmers Reproservice: Göteborg, 130-142.

AHRENDT, L. (1999): Säuglingsschwimmen. Studienergebnisse zur infektiös bedingten Krankheitshäufigkeit von Säuglingsschwimmkindern. In: STRASS, D./REISCHLE, K. (Hrsg.): Schwimmen 2000-III. Uehlin: Schopfheim, 173-180.

AHRENDT, L. (2000): Das Tauchen beim Säuglingsschwimmen. In: Sportpraxis 41 (1), 44-46.

AHRENDT, L. (2000): Das Tauchen beim Säuglingsschwimmen. In: DANIEL, K. (Red.): Symposiumsbericht zum 2. Kölner Schwimmsymposium 16./17.04.1999. Fahnemann: Bockenem.

AHRENDT, L. (2000): Motorische Frühstimulation durch Säuglingsschwimmen. Untersuchung der Wirkung regelmäßigen Wasseraufenthalts unter Berücksichtigung des mütterlichen Körperkonzepts. Uni. Diss.: Köln.

AYRES, J.A. (1992[2]): Bausteine der kindlichen Entwicklung. Springer: Berlin.

BAUERMEISTER, H. (1969, 1984[9]): In der Badewanne fängt es an. Wie kleine Kinder spielend schwimmen lernen. Copress: München.

BAUR, J./BÖS, K./SINGER, R. (Hrsg.) (1994): Motorische Entwicklung. Ein Handbuch. Schriftenreihe: Beiträge zur Lehre und Forschung im Sport; Bd. 106. Hofmann: Schorndorf.

BECK, E.G./SCHMIDT, P. (1994): Hygiene – Umweltmedizin. Enke: Stuttgart.

BRESGES, L./DIEM, L. (1972): Untersuchung zum Schwimmverhalten im ersten und zweiten Lebensjahr. Hofmann: Schorndorf, 20-28.

BRESGES, L. (1973): Schwimmen im 1. und 2. Lebensjahr. In: DIEM, L. (Hrsg.): Kinder lernen Sport. Bd. 1. Kösel: München.

BRESGES, L. (1972, 1981[2]): Schwimmen im ersten und zweiten Lebensjahr. In: DIEM, L. (Hrsg.): Kinder lernen Sport. Bd. 1. Kösel: München.

CAMUS, J. LE/MOULIN, J.-P./NAVARRO, C. (1994): L' enfant et l' eau. L' Harmattan: Paris.

CHEREK, R. (1984): Psycho- und sensomotorische Übungen im Wasser als Prävention und Rehabilitation (1.Teil). In: Krankengymnastik 36 (3), 157-164.

CHEREK, R. (1984): Psycho- und sensomotorische Übungen im Wasser als Prävention und Rehabilitation (2.Teil). In: Krankengymnastik 36 (4), 238-248.

CHEREK, R. (1998): Säuglings- und Kleinkinderschwimmen. Modernes Lernen: Dortmund.

DEUTSCHE LEBENSRETTUNGS-GESELLSCHAFT (DLRG) (Hrsg.): Erste Hilfe. Erkennen, Beurteilen, Handeln. DLRG: Bad Nenndorf.

DEUTSCHER SPORTÄRZTEBUND (Hrsg.) (1994): Stellungnahme Babyschwimmen. Textvorlage. DSÄB: Heidelberg.

DIEM, L. (1967): Ich bin – ich kann – ich will: Erfahrungen durch Bewegung. (Sonderdruck aus Leibeserziehung 11/ 1965). Hofmann: Schorndorf, 402-408.

DIEM, L./LEHR, U./OLBRICH, E./UNDEUTSCH, U. (1980): Längsschnittuntersuchung über die Wirkung frühzeitiger motorischer Stimulation auf die Gesamtentwicklung des Kindes im 4.-6. Lebensjahr. Schriftenreihe des Bundesinstituts für Sportwissenschaft; Bd. 31. Hofmann: Schorndorf.

DIN 19 643 – DEUTSCHES INSTITUT FÜR NORMUNG (Hrsg.): Aufbereitung von Schwimm- und Badebeckenwasser. Beuth Verlag: Berlin.

DYK, D. VAN (1996): Schwimmprogramme für Babies und Kleinkinder. (Video). Fahnemann: Bockenem.

EGGERT, D./SCHUCK, K.D. (1972): Untersuchungen zu Zusammenhängen zwischen Intelligenz, Motorik und Sozialstatus. Hofmann: Schorndorf.

GRAUMANN, D. (1996): Babyschwimmen. Pflesser: Flintbek.

HUNT-NEWMAN, V. (1967): Teaching an Infant to Swim. Hartcourt, Brace & World: New York.

HUNT-NEWMAN, V. (1967): So lernen kleine Kinder schwimmen. Goldmann: München.

JENNER, U. (2000): Eltern-Kind-Schwimmen im zweiten Lebensjahr. Untersuchung der Auswirkungen eines regelmäßigen Wasserprogramms auf Wasservertrautheit. Dipl. Arb.: Köln.

JÖKER, D. (Hrsg.): Das Krabbelmäuse Liederbuch. 100 quicklebendige Spiellieder. Menschenkinder Verlag.

KARCH, D. (Hrsg.) (1994): Risikofaktoren der kindlichen Entwicklung. (Klinik und Perspektiven). Steinkopff: Darmstadt.

KIPHARD, E.J. (1981): Sensomotorische Übungsbehandlung. In: CLAUSS, A. (Hrsg.): Förderung entwicklungsgefährdeter und behinderter Heranwachsender. (Beiträge zur Sportmedizin; Bd. 12). Perimed: Erlangen, 76-85.

KOCH, J. (1969): Der Einfluß der frühen Bewegungsstimulation auf die motorische und psychische Entwicklung des Säuglings. Sonderdruck aus: Bericht über den 26. Kongreß der Deutschen Gesellschaft für Psychologie (Hrsg.). Irle für Hogrefe: Göttingen.

KOCHEN, C./MCCABE, J. (1986): The Baby Swim Book. Leissure Press: Champaign.

KRAFFT, B. (1961): Widerstandsgymnastik mit Hilfe des Wasserauftriebes. In: Krankengymnastik 13 (11), 231-235.

KRAFFT, B. (1974): Die Auftriebstherapie und ihre Anwendung bei Coxarthrose. In: Krankengymnastik 26 (4), 123-126.

LIEDLOFF, J. (19992): Auf der Suche nach dem verlorenen Glück. Gegen die Zerstörung unserer Glücksfähigkeit in der frühen Kindheit. Beck: München.

LIETZ, R. (1993): Klinisch-neurologische Untersuchung im Kindesalter. Deutscher Ärzte-Verlag: Köln.

MAYERHOFER, A. (1952): Schwimmbewegungen bei Säuglingen. Univ. Diss.: Leipzig.

MAYERHOFER, A. (1953): Schwimmbewegungen bei Säuglingen. In: Archiv Kinderheilkunde 146, 137-142.

MCGRAW, M.B. (1939): Swimming Behavior of the Human Infant. In: J. Pediatrics Am. 15, 485-489.

MCGRAW, M.B. (1975): Growth. A Study of Jonny and Jimmy. Arno Press: New York.

MEINEL, K./ SCHNABEL, G. (1998⁹): Bewegungslehre – Sportmotorik: Abriß einer Theorie der sportlichen Motorik unter pädagogischen Aspekt. Sportverlag: Berlin.

MICHAELIS, R./NIEMANN, G. (1999): Entwicklungsneurologie und Neuropädiatrie. Hippokrates: Stuttgart.

MOULIN, J.-P. (1997): Pratiques aquatiques du jeune enfant et développement de l' autonomie. Etude longitudinale de l'influence des pratiques aquatiques sur le développement de l'autonomie de l'enfant, de l'âge de 9 mois à celui de 30 mois. Univ. Diss.: Toulouse.

MUMFORD, A.A. (1897): Survival Movements of the Human Infancy. In: Brain 20, pp. 285-294.

NUMMINEN, P./SÄÄKSLAHTI, A. (1994): Analysis on the Changes of Motor Activity in Infant Swimming. IN: Proceedings of the VII. International Symposium on Biomachanics and Medicine in Swimming. Atlanta (USA) 18.10.-23.10.94. Univ. Atlanta.

NUMMINEN, P./SÄÄKSLAHTI, A. (1998): Water as a Stimulant for Infants Motor Development. In: Proceedings of the VIII. International Symposium on Biomachanics and Medicine in Swimming. Jyväskylä (Finnland) 28.06.-02.07.98,. Univ. Jyväskylä, 102.

PAPOUSEK, H./PAPOUSEK, M. (1990): Intuitive elterliche Früherziehung in der vorsprachlichen Kommunikation. Teil I. In: Sozialpädiatrie 12 (7), 521-527.

PAPOUSEK, H./PAPOUSEK, M. (1990): Intuitive elterliche Früherziehung in der vorsprachlichen Kommunikation. Teil II. In: Sozialpädiatrie 12 (8), 579-585.

PIAGET, J. (1959, 1969, 1996[4]): Das Erwachen der Intelligenz beim Kinde. Gesammelte Werke 1. Studienausgabe. Klett-Cotta: Stuttgart.

PEIPER, A. (1961): Die Eigenart der kindlichen Hirntätigkeit. VEB Thieme: Leipzig.

PIGHIN, G./BRAUER, S. (1993): Das große Kinderförderprogramm. Pattloch: Augsburg.

PLIMPTON, C.E. (1986): Effects of Water and Land in Early Experience Programs on the Motor Development and Movement Comfortabbless of Infant Aged 6 to 18 Months. In: Perceptual and Motor Skills 62 (3), 719-728.

PORTMANN, A. (1972): Das extrauterine Frühjahr. In: HERZKA, H.ST. (Hrsg.): Das Kind von der Geburt bis zur Schule. Schwabe: Basel, 163-165.

POTACS, W. (1995): Grundzüge der Vojta-Therapie. Haug: Heidelberg.

PSCHYREMBEL (1998[258]): Klinisches Wörterbuch. De Guyter: Berlin.

RAABE-OETKER, A. (1998): Spiel und Spaß im Wasser – Babyschwimmen. Falken: Niedernhausen/Ts..

LARGO, R. (1998): Babyjahre. Die frühkindliche Entwicklung aus biologischer Sicht. Piper: München.

SCHILLING, F. (1973): Motodiagnostik im Kindesalter. Empirische Untersuchung an hirngeschädigten und normalen Kindern. Marhold: Berlin.

SCHMIDT-HANSBERG, M. (1981): Die Halliwick-Schwimm-Methode nach McMillan in der Rehabilitation Behinderter. In: Motorik 4 (3), 103-111.

SEILER, T. (1989): Erste Hilfe bei Säuglingen und Kindern. (Was Sie über akute, lebensbedrohliche Situationen und bei Unfällen wissen müssen, um schnell und richtig zu handeln). Thieme: Stuttgart.

SPITZ, R.A. (1967): Vom Säugling zum Kleinkind. Klett: Stuttgart.

WATSON, J.B. (1929): Psychology from the Standpoint of a Behaviorist. Lippincolt: Philadelphia.

WEIDINGER, G./KNYPHAUSEN, S. zu (1999[5]): Die schönsten und beliebtesten Kinderlieder zum Singen, Tanzen und Mitmachen. Cormoran: München.

WEIZSÄCKER, V. VON (1950): Der Gestaltkreis. Theorie der Einheit von Wahrnehmen und Bewegen. Thieme: Stuttgart.

WIELKI, C./HOUBEN, M. (1983): Descriptions of the Leg Movement of Infants in an Aquatic Environment. In: HOLLANDER, A.P. (Ed.): Biomechanics and Medicine in Swimming. International Series on Sport Science Vol. 14. Human Kinetics: Champaign, 66-71.

WILKE, K. (1990): Babyschwimmen. In: WILKE, K. (Hrsg.): Anfängerschwimmen. Rowohlt: Reinbek, 112-121.

WILMES-MIELENHAUSEN, B. (1994): Eltern-Kind-Gruppen. Herder Verlag: Freiburg i. Br..

ZINKE-WOLTER, P. (1994): Spüren – Bewegen – Lernen. Handbuch der mehrdimensionalen Förderung bei kindlichen Entwicklungsstörungen. Borgmann: Dortmund.

8 Alphabetical Index

Baby Swimming

Photo & Illustration Credits:

Cover Photo & Photos: Mathilde Kohl, Cologne
Illustrations: Markus Linden and Ulrike Bakiakas
Cover Design: Birgit Engelen